MW01706261

SELF LOVE CLUB, VOL. I

2020 MOMFIDENT AF Media

Cover Design - Christina Williams

ISBN: 978-1-7770177-1-2

For more information, visit www.GetMomfidentAF.com
or email hello@momfidentaf.com

#MOMFIDENTaf #MOMFIDENTaf MEDIA

This book is dedicated to the resiliency of women. We are strong, we are brave, and with a little support, we can get through anything.

This is for you, friend. Welcome to the Self Love Club.

Dear reader,

This book is a collaborative effort between Courtney St Croix, MOMFIDENT AF Media, and the Self-Love Club #AuthorSquad. We know you will see yourself in these pages, and there is nothing better than connecting with someone who just "gets it".

As you navigate each chapter, think about how you may reflect on every author's unique story, and use the space at the end of each chapter to record what stood out to you most clearly.

Share your takeaways on Instagram tagging both the author and @momfidentaf so we can see what parts resonate with you the most.

#SelfLoveClub

Contents

Introduction

Courtney St Croix

Have you ever gone through something in your life that was made a shit load easier when you found someone, *anyone,* who was going through the exact same thing as you? (Bonus points if it was at the exact same *time* as you?) This phenomenon is quite commonplace in the motherhood experience; not even just at this moment in time, but throughout history as we grew to realize that it truly does "take a village" and that, quite literally, it was a real and actual village that would help to raise our children. You know, those children born from families in said village. And now, in this modern motherhood experience, our "village" has become digital; creating helpful impact and connection for moms, despite often spanning large geographical distances. We have Facebook groups for any possible niche of motherhood struggle; there are millions of mommy-bloggers writing about their experiences and connecting with others going through the same things; there are Instagram accounts with massive communities of women just trying to do their best, and supporting each other as they do it. There are the friends you make by virtue of becoming a mom, and the friends you re-make by connecting with people you hadn't talked to for years, finding a relationship again due to your shared interest: motherhood.

I guess it makes sense for me to use motherhood as an example of something that women go through that is difficult, yet made a bit easier through connection, because I've spent the last several years focusing on helping moms build confidence through my brand, "MOMFIDENT AF." Either that, or, it's just a really simple and basic example that everyone can understand. It's one of those two justifications, definitely. But there are many other examples of "experiences" that you might go through that are made a "shit load easier" through connection with others going through the same thing. If you're going through a separation or a divorce; if you have suffered a specific loss; if you're planning a wedding; if you're working on a project with a few colleagues; if you are in the end zone of some kind of sports… something?[1] In any case, there are so many human experiences that are made better with other people sharing

---

1 I'm not great with the sports references… if you're competing for the Stanley Cup and it's like, really, really hard? I don't know. Don't hit me with your hockey stick for being a Canadian who barely knows hockey, eh?

them. That can be good things, too - it doesn't always have to be something you're struggling through. But struggle is difficult, and sharing difficult moments with others who "get it" help you get *through* it, a little bit easier.

This concept has been proven to me time and time again, when I've shared what I'm going through on social media and subsequently get an influx of incredible women commenting or privately messaging me to tell me they went though the *exact* same thing. Sometimes, they tell me how they got through it; other times they're in the middle of it, and are just offering their digital fist-bump as we both muddle through the difficulty. Sometimes, it brings a woman back to a time in her life, long ago, that she experienced the very same thing, and she is both sympathetic and supportive, despite being incredibly far away from what it is I'm going through. It. Is. Powerful. And I'm determined to re-create this over and over again so that more and more women can feel heard, seen, and understood.

As I'm writing this intro, I'm sitting at my kitchen table and my daughter is playing about 10 feet away from me. As a female entrepreneur who is also a mother to a busy four year old, sometimes my mom life is blended with my work life and I scrape five minutes together to accomplish a quick task. Sometimes, that task is promptly interrupted by someone asking me to get her a snack, come play Barbies, or help her find something that went missing (and is probably just, like, four inches to her left, out of her DIRECT gaze. Whatever, it makes me look like #supermom when I come to the rescue and **gasp** find whatever it was she lost, so, that's okay.) I'm sure if you're a mother reading this, whether you own a business or not, you can relate. You know, trying to accomplish something with littles boppin' about is difficult. Big time. You could just be trying to throw in a flippin' load of laundry and someone comes tugging at your shirt. As mothers, we regularly put our own needs behind everybody else's, and our intentions are pure. We want to take care of everybody else. It's natural for us. We *want* to play Barbies with our kids at that first innocent request, but sometimes we need to empty the damn dishwasher so we can then go about making dinner and having clean plates to do so, and we can't always appease everyone else's needs *right* this second. (Or, maybe you *don't* really want to play Barbies. No judgement, I actually am not one of those moms who loves "playing" either.) But for a large percentage of your time, my guess is you *are* trying to please everybody else first. You *do* put other people ahead of yourself, regularly. You *aren't* heavily prioritizing your own self-care and subsequently, building your self-love portfolio. Maybe you're just surviving.

If you resonated at all with anything I just mentioned above, then you've proved my theory right there. We. Are. Connected. With motherhood and parenting; with struggling to work and take care of your family; with struggling to handle being a stay-at-home-mom with multiple children; with experiencing a negative body image; with the constant lurking of mom guilt; with feeling less-than or never-good-enough; with constantly comparing ourselves to others; with struggling to maintain a healthy mindset along with your healthy lifestyle… we are all connected. And connection is what truly helps us to navigate the muddy waters of this complicated (and beautiful) life.

I've shed many a tear while reading through the stories you're about to hear from this incredibly talented and diverse group of women. Sometimes, I cried because I could completely relate to what they are sharing and what they went through. Other times, it was because I couldn't relate, and I practiced immense empathy for what they have experienced and how they worked hard to overcome their struggle. Each story is littered with lessons of self-love strategies, and these women are dealing with some seriously important themes. Grief, loss, alcoholism, infertility, weight loss, motherhood, childhood trauma, fitness culture, mental decluttering, self-help, body hair, conformity, self-acceptance, societal standards, isolation, PCOS, insecurities, fears, doubts, anxiety, depression, suicide, personal identity, body image, external expectations, judgement, criticism, bullying…all of these themes (and more!) are included in these pages. This project is a labour of love and I know that it has the power to shape how you view your own story by virtue of being a part of theirs.

At the start of each chapter, you'll get an intro to the author you're about to hear from. You'll also see some contact information and I urge you to connect and reach out to these women should you feel called to share where their words have reached you and made an imprint on your life. They say it takes a village to raise a child, but I truly think it takes a village to just be a woman in this world, and to get through the difficulty of healing that is often required as we make our way towards our own version of self-love. Or at least, it's a whole lot easier and more supportive with a village around you. Welcome to ours. It's a club, and everybody is welcome.

You can sit with us.

You know where to find me. If you want to reach out about how this project has helped you, or are interested in contributing to a future project, find me on Instagram @ momfidentaf or at **getmomfidentaf.com**, and let's talk.

PART I:

Going Through It

Self-Love Realizations Through Fertility, Body Image, Grieving, Loss, and Failure

CHAPTER ONE

Adrienne Wanless-Aitken

Adrienne Wanless-Aitken is an Emotional Intelligence Coach, e-learning Designer and Independent Zyia Active Representative who is passionate about helping busy moms impact how they show up as their best selves, moving from a place of love, and creating online courses. Adrienne has been working in the fitness industry since 1999 and for the past fifteen years has focused on leadership development and coaching within the corporate fitness world. She has a passion for helping busy moms navigate their emotions, and become intentional with their work, personal, and family relationships. She enjoys Crossfit, hanging out with her husband and six-year-old twins, spending time with friends and family, and hot summer days.

Find Adrienne: @adrienne.simplyintentional
www.besimplyintentional.com

I have struggled with my body image for as long as I can remember. I can almost pin-point the moment I looked at myself and went from a happy, carefree, athletic, chatty nine-year-old to instantly confused and disgusted about the body I was in. Before this moment, I didn't really think much about my body. Other than the fact that I loved how it moved. I loved how flexible it was, I loved that I could do multiple back walkovers in a row without getting dizzy. I loved how I could see the definition in my arms and legs when I moved. One day, one comment, and everything changed. I was 10.

I remember starting to hear my mom constantly speak about her new "diet" she was on and how she "needed" to lose weight and honestly, I thought it was annoying and rude that she would talk about herself that way. Maybe she had always done this, but for some reason I started to become more aware of how negatively she spoke about herself. I started to wonder what the fuss was all about, because I didn't care what she looked like, so why was she worrying about it so much? Every meal she would mention her "points," whatever that meant, and every meal she would declare what she could and couldn't eat like it was an announcement we should all take note of. I ignored it, but wondered if she needed a reminder that we *loved her just the way she was*. I was confused. If she changed her size, what would be different? Then, I started to become aware of how my dad was commenting on her food. "Are you going to eat that? Is that on your diet? How much weight have you lost? Do you really think you should be eating that?" Huh, interesting. So, I came to the conclusion that how you look is apparently important to others, and how you look to others seems to matter in a big way. It's possible that my dad always did this, but this is when I really started to notice.

Around the age of ten, my body really started changing, because I was going through *puberty* for crying out loud! I was getting boobs! This was, as I learned, sort of an inconvenience to someone who enjoyed sports as much as I did. Especially because I played sports with boys. They started to look at me in a way I had never seen before. I was beyond annoyed by this. Oversized sweaters became my new favourite attire! Shortly after my boobs 'arrived,' I got my period, and then everything started to change. But the exact moment, that *very first* moment I felt ashamed and disgusted about my body, was one night at gymnastics practice. My coach, who was a very strong, somewhat intimidating, serious Russian man, said to me: "You better do something about your fat ass or you won't be able to swing on those bars for very much longer." He turned to my dad and said I needed to lose some weight. I wanted to die. I wanted to scream. I wanted to cry.

Not that I need to clarify that this is a terrible thing to say to *anyone*, let alone a ten-year-old, but I feel it's important that you know: when I look back at the photos of my competitive gymnastic years, I was not even the *slightest* bit fat. I was strong, I was muscular, I was brave...and I was happy. I was fit and proud of how I moved. There is no way, not even a shred, of fat on my body. But, from that moment on, I believed I was fat, and frankly, disgusting. In that *exact*, burned-in-my-brain moment, I started to believe that I had to change how I looked to be worthy of attention, love and acceptance. I believed that someone else's opinion of my body, *MY* FREAKING BODY, mattered. I believed that what I looked like on the outside was somehow more import then who I was on the inside.

I spent the next 27 years of my life hating my body. Not just disliking it, or disappointed in my strong legs, and broad shoulders, I legitimately *hated* my body. During the time I went through high school, I developed a terrible relationship with food. I was either not eating, or binging and purging. I was constantly being forced to finish every last bite on my plate at the dinner table (because you know, you can't waste food), and this led to me become constantly terrified I would gain an ounce. After every meal, I would sneak off to the bathroom and shove my fingers down my throat. This always ended with me in tears on the bathroom floor, until my brother (who I'm sure will not be shocked to find out his back-then suspicions were true) would knock on the door and say "Adrienne, are you okay? You don't sound good. Did you just, ummm, were you just sick?" Every single time I would say, "I am fine, just leave me alone."

In my twenties, after gaining twenty pounds from college, I began to obsessively workout. Three to five hours a week quickly turned into 20-25 hours of exercise per week. I lost those 20 pounds and then I lost 20 more. I was down to 17 percent body fat. There were moments that I loved my body. Sometimes, I felt like I was that nine-year-old girl who could take on the world again. And then someone would comment about my muscular arms, saying things like: "Nobody wants a girl who looks too muscular" or "You look like a guy." And I would revert back to what I always did, I would sit back in the comfortable pattern of hating my body. I took weight loss pills and went back and forth from purging to obsessing over EVERY SINGLE CALORIE that went into my mouth. If only I looked like the models did, I would think.

***

When I met my (now) husband Todd, I was in a pretty good place. One year single after a dysfunctional relationship, I finished college and was working as a Massage Therapist at a women's only fitness club. I was happy, I was healthy, I was eating fairly well, I was training for a marathon, and I was somewhat respecting my body. Todd and I started talking on the phone obsessively, and we discovered that we both enjoyed movement and exercise. I quickly convinced him to go on long Sunday runs with me (and I'm 100% certain he hated every single step, but he did it anyway). Over the first year we travelled back and forth to see each other and the weekends always involved some sort of workout together. Running in the woods, weight lifting, or a cycling class. I was in a good place mentally and was no longer purging as a form of "weight control." I would still obsess about my weight, but my head was distracted by my heart most of the time.

Another year of a long distance relationship went by and we finally decided it was time to move in together. I left my friends and my job, now as the manager of a women's only fitness club, and moved to the big ~~city~~ town of Port Perry. I loved it. I eventually started working as the manager of a large fitness chain, and I felt like I was on top of the world. I was living with the love of my life, I was working at a job I loved and I was meeting new people and forming new friendships. Yet, I would still look in the mirror and wish I was skinnier, and wish that my body looked different in some way. I would still set goals that centred around losing weight. If I did happen to lose some weight, I had friends and acquaintances who would comment that I looked "sick" or "too fit" or "overly muscular" and this fed my belief that I had to change my exterior body to gain acceptance from others. Now let that sink in for a second. I felt I had to change my exterior body to gain acceptance from others...and in turn, myself. Working in the fitness industry meant that we were always talking about goals, setting goals, talking to others about setting goals, telling others to set goals, then setting more goals. Our business model was (and is) built on pushing others to want to change how they look. It's built on forcing others to see their body as something they can mold and change into something better. It is built on the idea that if you get people to feel pain and show them the pleasure, you can get them to buy hope.

Now, let me be clear. I am not naïve. I know this is a business model that has worked in the sales industry for decades. Get your customer to feel the pain of not having something they really want, then show them what it would be like if they had it or achieved it, then dangle the carrot of hope in front of them so they will buy. It's a popular model and it works. At the time I was selling memberships, though, I believed I was helping people "get healthy" by making them feel bad enough about themselves that they would want to change. And you know what? I was really good at it. So good in fact, I turned my club from an unsuccessful, underperforming facility, to a top performing one. I was nominated for manager of the year, twice! I was obsessed with setting goals and crushing them. I also want to note that I was good at other things too, like building and maintaining relationships with my team, and I did *genuinely* care about helping others. But when I look back and think about why I was so good at getting people to that place of "pain," that place where they would sit in front of me in tears, feeling disgusted about their bodies and thinking that just a little exercise would fix it all... I realize I was good at this because I *was* them. All the time. I believed the only way to everlasting happiness was to hit the magic number on the scale and BAM, the sky would open up and all would be perfect. It is both incorrect and damaging to think this way, and to lead others to think this way.

In a perfect world, the fitness industry would simultaneously support people to use fitness as a way to move their body to get healthy, while they also get education for their mindset on what getting "healthy" looks and feels like on the inside. You sign up at a gym, you get a personal trainer and a mindset coach, and they work together to teach you about fitness for health versus fitness for looks. Either way, I believe, setting goals about your health *is* necessary to maintaining a happy thriving life, but your health isn't just about how you look.

***

Years passed, Todd and I got married, and we bought our first house together. We were planning to have kids, we were happy, and for the first time I could picture my future life with someone amazing. We would have two, maybe three (or four!) kids, we would raise them to enjoy movement, we would travel with them, teach them to kind and well-adjusted adults, and maybe one day we would have grandkids.

The first year of trying to conceive was difficult. So I came up with a plan. I made it my mission to see a doctor, get the tests, find the "problem" and of course, fix it. Set the goal, work at it, and achieve it. This is how life works, right? I was pretty good at crushing goals. As it would turn out, infertility was a different story, and was a word I eventually got very used to saying. I wouldn't dare discuss this with others, with friends, or family. First of all, what would they say? Would they look at me with pity or would they offer me advice, as if to imply I wasn't trying everything in the book? Or maybe they would look at me the way I did, like I was broken or like I needed to be "fixed" in some way.

The fact that I was already in the mindset of not liking my body made this infertility diagnoses only confirm that my body was dysfunctional. It confirmed exactly how much I hated my body for not looking a certain way and now, for not functioning the way it should. I hated that every month when I peed on a stick, I wasn't pregnant. I hated that everyone around me was having babies so easily and I wasn't. I hated that we wanted to have kids and nothing was happening. I hated every treatment we tried. Every tincture, every acupuncture appointment, every IUI, every needle I would jam into my thigh or stomach, every bruise I would get from the needles. I hated all the travelling to appointments, every early morning appointment before work, every test and re-test they would perform on Todd and I; I hated every IVF treatment and when there was no baby at the end of it, I cried so hard. I hated that I faked every smile and congratulations to every friend and family member who had a baby in their arms when we didn't. I looked in the mirror every day for five years, and I hated my body even more than I ever had. I was secretly depressed. I am sure my close friends and family started to recognize how withdrawn I became, but since my motto always was "Fake it 'til you make it!" I tried my hardest to distract myself and pull it together daily.

I started to gain weight. I gained 20 pounds during my

five years trying to conceive (TTC). I always maintained my workout routine, but I would eat my feelings most of the time and my hormones were completely out of whack for sure. We switched clinics (again), only this time we got to fly to Barbados for our IVF treatment. Beautiful, sunny, warm Barbados. "This time it will work," we'd say. This time our $12,000 will be money well spent. This time, I got pregnant. I have never felt like crying and smiling so much at the same time, ever. To this day, never have I felt the way I did that day I took the pregnancy test and discovered I was pregnant! WHAT THE!? This was it. We were finally, after five long years, we were having a baby.

Four weeks later, we lost our baby.

At this point, I hated every inch of my skin with all of my heart. I was in a dark place. Weeks went by, and I couldn't stand how much pain was in emotionally so I did what I thought was healthy, of course: I ran. I ran until my physical pain took over my emotional pain because this is how I always coped with my emotional pain. I started my hard core workouts again. I began to obsess about my food and my weight. I put my energy into something I could control: how much weight I could lose. I got to a place where I was the healthiest I had felt in a long time.

We decided we would give IVF one more shot, and go down the road of appointments, hormones, and being poked and prodded, just one more time. If this didn't work, we would call it quits and accept our fate. We would go back to Barbados, enjoy our three weeks in the sun, and hope that there would be a baby in the end. One week after we arrived home, we found out we were expecting triplets. We were terrified and excited all at the same time. Three freakin' babies! Not just one, but *three*! I was elated

We quickly found out that one baby was not going to make it. I was immediately concerned about this pregnancy, considering what happened last time. The nurse explained that the other two heart beats were strong and told us to stay positive. Over the next seven months, I barely slept. I was terrified something bad was going to happen. I had ultrasound after ultrasound, plus many tests and checkups. I was a high-risk pregnancy and they were monitoring everything carefully. I would tell my body every day to keep these two babies alive; to please, *please,* finally do something right.

I enjoyed growing humans inside me, but I am sad to say that I was not happy with my body. I never stopped to appreciate what it had gone through to get to this point. I didn't appreciate the beauty of pregnancy and thank it for hanging on for so long while I tortured it with needles and tests and treatments. On October 31, 2013, when our boy/girl twins were born, we were so in love with them. Months went by of living off of two-hour sleep intervals and I hadn't thought of anything but sleeping, wanting sleep, how to get more sleep, how to get the babies to sleep and when I would ever sleep for 5 hours again.

Well, at least I wasn't obsessing over my body and how it looked, for once.

Five months into our new lives together, when I started sleeping for 4-5 hours a night, I started to come alive again. My eyes were fuzzy and my brain was a little less foggy. And, naturally, my priority became obsessing about "getting my body back".

***

Around the time my twins were nearly three years old, my daughter asked me a simple question that brought me to tears. "Mommy, why do you exercise?" (Well, it sounded more like "Mama, why you x-sa-sise?" but I knew what she meant.) I mean, just a regular question, right? Well, I guess not for me. Why I worked out was not something I was expecting to explain to my kids. At least not at this age.

I had started back to my semi-regular workouts when the twins were almost five months. Sometimes, that would look like me working out in the living room during nap time, or attempting to, and like clockwork, one or both of them would wake up, so I would hold one or both and do squats or lay them on the ground and do pushup-kisses... definitely a favourite in our house. Sometimes, if I was feeling feisty and brave, I would pack 17 diapers and 12 extra pairs of clothes in a bag and head to the gym where I would attempt to walk on the treadmill, ride a bike or do some core work for about 16 minutes, just so I could shove them back on my boob and frantically try and get home so they would nap again. #momlife. By the time they had turned two years old, they knew exactly what exercise looked like, and they knew that mommy worked for a fitness club. They might have actually thought my job was just to work out all day long. The question "why do you work out" has always been something I could answer quite quickly to any onlooker, especially when I worked as a gym manager. "I'm training for a marathon" or "I want to lose weight" became easy answers that no one would dispute, and I always had an answer. But when my kids asked me this question it felt different. They wanted the truth. And the truth was, well, ugly.

I wasn't ready to tell them: "Well, kids, Mommy has always hated how she looked." I wasn't ready to say that Mommy was ten years old when someone told her that she needed to lose weight because her hips and butt were bigger than the other gymnasts. I wasn't ready to explain that a boy at school called me thunder thighs when I was eleven and that made me start to think terrible thoughts about how I looked. I didn't want to explain why I had been in constant pursuit of changing my body to look a certain way, thinking I would please others and win the happiness award if I could *just* be skinner. I didn't want to tell them that at age fourteen I would spend more time in the bathroom than I did playing with my friends, and around the age of seventeen I started taking chemical-filled diet pills. It made me sad to have to explain that because of all that, when I was 20 I became obsessive about external change, spending up to 25 hours each week working out intensely. How could I tell them this? How could I let them know that Mommy worked out because she actually *hated* how she felt in her own skin, and thought it was necessary to change her exterior in order to love herself? How could I tell them that after a close friend got engaged and everyone was talking about how to "lose weight before the wedding" that she went right back to her old habits? How could I tell them that my relationship with my own body, the one that carried them to term and birthed the most precious little beans, was a sick and sad one?

This is when I realized my first trigger. Talking about, or thinking about, losing weight. How ironic for someone who had made a living on talking to others about their fitness goals and ultimately...how to lose weight! I quickly realized that stress, was also a trigger for my eating disorder or disordered eating. Instead of telling my kids all of this nasty, messy, and complicated history (of which they would not understand anyway) I told them what I wanted the answer to be. I told them what I would want their answer to be. I told them a lie.

"Mommy works out because she loves herself," I said, as I sobbed and gave them both a hug. "Mommy, loves herself so much that she wants to be healthy, strong and have energy to be able to pick you up and run after you!" I said this as I quickly changed my mood and chased them giggling down the hall of our house. This answer stirred around in my head for weeks after I told them. Now, how do I actually make this a truth? How do I actually step into this and love myself. Why did I need to make this a truth and not just something I *told* my kids? Because, I have a daughter. One day her body will change, someone will say something to her that will feel like it actually matters what they think about her and her body. I did not want her to be me. I did not want her to think she wasn't worthy, that she didn't deserve love until she was a number on a scale.

And because also, I have a son. I have a son who will one day grow up and live in this world with other women. His sister, his cousins, friends, aunts and his mom, and other women who regularly struggle with their body image, and I want him to know that no matter what size a women is she is worthy of love and kindness. I want him to know that he does not get to comment on a woman's body and tell her she needs to be something else. Thinner, curvier, more or less muscular, bigger boobs, smaller boobs...whatever. I want him to know that none of that matters in the end. What matters is who people are on the inside.

I knew I had to change my perspective...I just wasn't sure how.

A few weeks passed, and I stopped by one of the fitness clubs in my region. I brought some treats for the manager. She had been working so hard the last couple months and her and her team were about to have a long couple of days to close out her month. I bumped into a senior manager and in true Adrienne fashion, I wanted to share. I asked her if she wanted a cupcake. She proceeded to give me a long-winded explanation of how she most definitely could *not* have a cupcake, because she needed to watch her already very slender 110 pound figure and was completely off sugar because she needed to lose the 3 pounds she gained on her holidays. Now, while I know it is okay to have goals to be a healthier version of yourself, this answer in particular set me over the top. I must have glared a hole through her body that very instance. Trigger number three, apparently, is other people talking about their weight, how much weight they have to lose, or their specific calorie intake at any given moment.

I politely said goodbye and drove straight to a CrossFit gym and signed one year membership. This was my first step into self-acceptance. If you have ever been to a CrossFit gym, you know that the environment is very different than a typical "gym". This is not an advertisement for CrossFit, but it was the exact environment and community that I needed heal, because it is one that focuses *away* from weight loss or what you look like in a pair of jeans, and more about your personal records, your strength gains, you showing up, and getting through the workout and others cheering you on as you try not to look like you are dying while you do it. After three workouts, I knew this was where I would change that lie I told my kids, into the truth.

Fast forward to the launch of MOMFIDENT AF in 2017. This was when I actually started to focus on how to change the narrative in my head. Courtney has always been someone I admire. When she re-branded into MOMFIDENT AF, it just seemed to make sense. Courtney was the only person that I ever remember schooling me for talking smack about my body. We were at a fitness conference together (and this was likely in 2008-2009) and we just finished a workout with another colleague. As I looked around at all the beautifully sculpted bodies, I casually said, "I *so* need to lose 10 pounds." For context, I was at least 30 pounds less than I am right now as I write this. I worked out five to six times a week and my body fat was around 19%. I didn't NEED to lose 10 pounds by any means, but this is what I always told myself and so, it's what I always thought. Courtney looked at me and said with a very stern look on her face, "I can't believe you would say that about yourself and I am actually really mad right now. I look up to you and I am really upset to find out that you talk about yourself that way." The disappointment she had in me that day is something I will never forget. At the time, I didn't have the tools to change, so when MOMFIDENT AF launched, I knew I had to follow along.

I was on a mission to self-acceptance. To make my lie become a reality. I worked my way up to going to CrossFit four times a week. I started listening to The Momfidence Podcast. I unfollowed people on social media that were not aligned with my values, and I started following people who were. I did my self-love journal daily. I started reading books about self-confidence. I completed any activities Courtney suggested. I searched for more activities that I could implement to shift my perspective or my body. I was beginning to believe that I loved my body. I practiced every day when I looked at myself in the mirror, saying one thing I loved about my body. I would smile, and I would feel it.

I was there. I loved my body for what it was and what it does for me.

Then one day, my kids brought home a Mother's Day card form school. It had a bunch of questions that they had answer about me, their mom. Their teacher helped them fill it out. At first I thought this was cute. Then I saw this question at the bottom "How much does your mom weigh?"

Now the answers were hilarious which were at least entertaining. My daughter's answer was, well, hurtful at first, my son's answer made me want to kiss him. Then I thought, how is this an important question to who I am as their mother, as a women, as a person? I quickly brushed it off and gave them a big smooch and moved on with the rest of the Mother's Day loving. Later that night, I couldn't help but wonder when will we (as a society and as women on this planet), put a stop to girls' and women's bodies being the topic of conversation? When will we stop thinking that it is okay or that it's somehow important how much you weigh in the grand scheme of things? When will this stop being the topic of conversations we have with each other and about others?

This is where you come in, where we all come in. It's a team effort. It has to be. Start with yourself first.

I can't go back to tell that ten-year-old girl how beautiful she was, how worthy she was of love and acceptance for the body she was given; I can't go back and tell her that her muscular legs and defined shoulders do not make her look less feminine but rather like a strong BADASS girl who will take on the world one day. I can't go back and tell her that what she looks like on the outside isn't as important as who she is on the inside. Truthfully, I am okay with that, I have healed from that pain.

What I want, is for us to be aware of how we talk to ourselves, either inside our head or aloud. I want us to be aware of how we talk about our bodies, girl's bodies, anyone's bodies, especially around the little girls in our lives. We need to show them, dammit we need to *tell* them, shout it from the roof tops, that the size on the scale or the size of your jeans does not determine your worth. You are more than what you look like on the outside. I will always strive to move my body in a way that makes me feel strong and fuel my body so I have the energy to do so but aiming for that "perfect" size isn't part of my narrative, my goals, or my life anymore.

What I know right now, in this moment, is that I am beautiful, I am strong, I am worthy and enough as I am today. And so are you sister, girlfriend, mama, sweet beautiful child. SO. ARE. YOU!

KEY TAKEAWAY

Adrienne Wanless-Aitken

@adrienne.simplyintentional
@momfidentaf
#selfloveclub

CHAPTER TWO

Maggie Callaghan

Maggie is a mother, wife, Yoga Instructor, Fertility Support Practitioner, writer, and lover of life from Oshawa, Ontario, Canada. Maggie's wellness journey began when she started practicing yoga during a time when she didn't quite feel like herself. As the love for her yoga practice grew, she decided to take a yoga teacher certification and hasn't looked back since. During her family planning, Maggie struggled with infertility and went through some confusing, difficult challenges as she tried to become a mother. She was luckily blessed, and after the birth of her daughter, she decided she wanted to learn everything she could about fertility health. She started her business and began teaching yoga exclusively. Now, Maggie offers a variety of services for women including Fertility Support and Education. She focuses on using yoga and body awareness to uplift women on all paths of life. By blending yoga and fertility support into one, Maggie is on a mission to change the face of infertility in a positive way.

Find Maggie: @femme.fertility
Author Photo: Adriana Wilkin Photography

I never thought I would have a problem getting pregnant.

Growing up, I never knew what infertility was. This was not a phrase I had ever heard of, and I can still remember my aunts and mum talking about the day I would have my own babies. In school, I can remember all the times I was told how easy it would be to get pregnant and how to avoid pregnancy at all costs, so when it came time for family planning, I figured it would only take one or two cycles before I was pregnant. I felt like our family would be expanding within the year, so you could imagine my surprise when after a year of actively trying, my doctor said it was time to see the fertility doctor.

Leaving the doctor's office was a trip. It was hard enough going through that first year as it was. Every month I had a late period or my body felt off, I was convinced I was pregnant. To now be told I should see a fertility doctor was a particularly hard pill to swallow and I felt way out of my element. Amazingly enough, a few days after this appointment, I found out we were pregnant so we didn't actually have to follow through with the fertility doctor. The day I found out, I planned a surprise announcement for my husband when we got home from work. I remember getting the first ultrasound done and thinking about all the things I was going to love and enjoy during my pregnancy. I remember telling many of my close friends early on because I was just too excited.

I was at work when I first noticed the spotting. I immediately Googled what that could mean, and as anyone knows, that's literally the worst thing you can do. I read an article on my pregnancy app that talked about spotting and how it can be normal, so I figured this was the case with me. I tried not to think about it. At this point, I didn't even think that something could go wrong and so I figured, "Out of sight, out of mind." The next day, there was still spotting, but again, nothing I thought was concerning. On the third day, I noticed bright red blood and I knew. I remember feeling panicked as I was calling my doctor who advised me to go to the hospital. My husband was trying to remain calm and comforting as we made our way to the hospital. As emotionally unprepared as I was for the possibility having fertility issues, I was even more unprepared for suffering a miscarriage. I remember sitting in the emergency room, anger already setting in along with despair. I was crying – actually, I was sobbing and hyperventilating - and I didn't care who was watching. I didn't even end up being seen by a doctor or having it confirmed by a urine test which they still hadn't completed. I was so messed up from miscarrying in front of everyone in the emergency room that I just wanted to get home. It was the worst day of my life.

The days, weeks and months that followed were difficult. I swore I wasn't going to try getting pregnant again. I resented my body and treated it like a piece of garbage, which is how I felt about it at the time. There was a lot of blame there. I began to avoid my friends with babies, especially the ones who were pregnant at the same time I was. I ran away from my yoga mat and lived in sadness. Everything made me cry. I eventually got to a point where I knew I needed help, and so I ended up speaking with a therapist. Three months later, I was ready to try getting pregnant again.

This time around, we did see a fertility doctor. It was interesting to me that when I first met with the doctor, there wasn't any real discussion in regards to the root cause of my infertility. I was told to take a prescribed medication and within six months, I'd be pregnant. The medication basically forced ovulation, and for the first time in my life, my cycles were 28 days, spot on. During this particular part of my motherhood journey, I was getting blood work done twice a month at the fertility clinic. One time was to test my progesterone to ensure ovulation had occurred, and the second time was to confirm pregnancy. I would get up at 5:00 am, drive to the clinic for 6:00 am, have blood work taken, and then wait for a phone call with my results. If my progesterone levels were raised, there was optimism that it meant a positive pregnancy test would be coming my way two weeks later. This went on for 5 months. I was on my last dose of medication and really had come to terms with the fact that this might not happen for me.

I remember the day I found out I was pregnant again. I got up to get ready for the clinic, and when I went to the bathroom, I felt off. Something was different. I grabbed a home pregnancy test I had and, lo and behold, it was positive. This is the exact moment that fear consumed my entire body. Of course, the clinic confirmed the pregnancy and booked my first ultrasound for me. This time around, there was no surprise announcement to my husband. It was simply a text message saying, "I'm pregnant." We didn't tell any friends or family. I wasn't even excited. I was so scared that things were going to end badly again and so I didn't want to do anything to jinx it. I left my toxic work environment, started a new job, and just tried to enjoy being pregnant.

Naturally, pregnancy was difficult for me. I was sick from weeks six through twenty-two. It was constant and some days were worse than others. I ended up telling my mum about my pregnancy because she knew I was off with being as sick as I was. I couldn't drive because I was constantly throwing up, and being stuck in traffic on a busy highway for hours at a time while throwing up is not a fun experience. I broke out in head-to-toe hives for three days, and each day, I felt like I was experiencing a hangover. I was also riddled with guilt for not being happy or excited about the pregnancy. As the days went on and my belly grew, so did all my insecurities about my body. I didn't have a scale or a full-length mirror in my home for a long time. It was just never something my husband and I used often, so for a while, I didn't know what my full pregnant body looked like. I only knew I was getting stretch marks on my hips and my belly had started to pop. About the time of my baby shower I went shopping for an outfit to wear. I was rocking leggings and the same Blue Jays T-shirt most days and so I wanted to look like the glowing pregnant woman everyone talks about. My mum and I went together, and that was the first time I had seen my new body since becoming pregnant. I had a meltdown. I bawled my face off in the change room of the maternity clothing store and it was the ugliest cry you have ever witnessed. I couldn't stop staring at the crazy amount of stretch marks on the front of my belly. My legs looked massive and had stretch marks everywhere. Something that should have been a happy experience had suddenly escalated and turned into a moment of self-loathing and total disgust with my appearance, quickly followed by more guilt. What kind of mother and woman am I to be so trivial about my appearance? I'm growing a human inside of me and it's a miracle - I should be more grateful! Truthfully, I was grateful. Despite all these things going on, my pregnancy was healthy. I didn't have complications and my babe was growing like she was supposed to be. The change room incident wasn't the only time I fought with my body and my appearance. At twenty-one weeks, the round ligament pain I had was awful. Every movement I made hurt, but at the time, every medical professional I had talked to said it was normal and so I believed them. I tried to get back into yoga, but it had been so long since I had done a practice, the immediate relief I was looking for was not within reach. By twenty-eight weeks, my babe was already in the optimal birth position and the immense pressure I felt on my pubic bone was awful. I found myself hunching over a lot, unable to sit or stand for long periods of time, and my feet were beyond swollen. I kept thinking to myself, "Why is this my experience?" Why was my whole body a vessel I no longer knew and why couldn't I accept or love the changes happening to my body?

My due date came and went with no signs of babe coming, so I was induced a week later. I hadn't created a birth plan and basically told the doctors and nurses to do whatever was necessary to bring my child in to the world safely. My labour was slow and agonizing. I had a fever, I was throwing up constantly, and my epidural had briefly run out at one point so things got a little crazy. After twenty-two hours, I was so exhausted from labour. We were told that I was stuck at nine centimetres and showed no signs of going any further, so after another four hours, it was finally decided that a caesarean was necessary. That experience was also very traumatic for me. When my daughter was delivered, she didn't cry or scream in the way they expected or hoped, and so she was sent up to the NICU. My husband followed her up there while I went to recovery. I had some clotting issues and laid in recovery for three hours after my surgery. During that time, I had no idea what was going on with my daughter and I was in the most excruciating pain I've ever experienced. Finally, my husband joined me and filled me in on what was going on with Sawyer. She joined us about an hour later and I was finally moved into a recovery room with my precious baby girl. Our new life was set to begin.

Getting out of the hospital and into our new routine

was the best feeling. I felt good, all things considered, and was super relieved that we had the green light to head home after only three days in the hospital. The first couple of weeks at home were an interesting time as we adjusted to having a newborn baby. In addition to our daily routine changing, I was also dealing with more changes to my body. My maternity clothes stopped fitting, but I couldn't get into my pre-pregnancy clothes either. I told myself it was time to start getting back into exercise and yoga. My daughter was two months old when I started exercising again and I bought clothes that were a smaller size as motivation to lose weight. I didn't keep up with working out for long because I developed chronic back pain from postural issues and pelvic floor muscle issues from being pregnant, and so I realized I had to take it easy. I was okay with that, honestly. I figured, "I just had a baby. I have time."

About a week or so later, I was in my room with my daughter and I was getting dressed. She was laying on the bed and I was looking at myself in the new full-length mirror I had bought. I was in a Smash and Tess romper that I had only worn a couple of times. It was a little form fitting, and so it hugged my belly and really showed my curves. I had never been bothered by it before, but on that day, it triggered every insecurity and limiting belief about myself and I felt like I was the most disgusting, hideous human being in the world. It was such a bad day I asked my husband to take her while I finished getting ready. I was so disgusted in how this piece of clothing fit, I literally ripped it from my body. Grabbed the sleeves, became the

Incredible Hulk and ripped a piece of clothing off my body. I put on my trusty leggings and baggy top, picked up the pieces of romper off the floor and walked to my kitchen to throw it out. I felt so much shame and sadness and couldn't understand why my body wasn't the way I wanted it to be. It was in that moment, I knew what I was feeling about my body was dangerous and unhealthy and things needed to change. I knew I had to be better for my daughter, I knew I never wanted her to feel how I was feeling in that moment and I knew I deserved better.

After deciding to make a change, things and people began to appear in my path that would come to support me in my healing in more ways than one. The first major thing to happen was I decided I didn't want to go back to work in a traditional sense and instead wanted to get back to teaching yoga and finally open the studio I've always dreamed about. This was a pretty big declaration on my part, but I was determined to have the life I wanted – a life I thought would be the best for Sawyer. I stepped back on my mat and began using poses to help support my body in healing. Slowly, my back pain stopped and I started to feel normal again. I invested in myself and worked with a coach for the first time. This experience allowed me to learn about limiting beliefs and self-worth, fear, and getting clear about how I wanted to feel in life and business. Around this same time, I also found body positive women to follow on social media and began a gratitude practice. I started to journal a lot more. I started to listen to podcasts and read spiritual books. When the program with my coach finished six weeks later, I was clear on who I wanted to be and how I wanted to feel in life and business. I decided that I wanted to support women using yoga. Once that decision was made, things really exploded.

I had decided to launch my social media pages for my business once I finished my course. I had this Instagram page I had created years ago to document my personal yoga practice, but I was always so scared of judgement and had major impostor syndrome that I would come to delete the photos from this page more than once. I had kept the page open, so I changed it to a business page and just kept posting. I kept pushing myself to do the things that made me uncomfortable because I knew the discomfort I felt wasn't me—it was the stories I believed about myself. I would never know if someone actually judged me. I wouldn't know if they thought I was a fraud. The only thing I knew was I had to keep going. The more I shared on social media the more things popped up in my life to support me in healing.

I remember sitting at my computer thinking about what services I would offer in my yoga business when the idea to offer yoga for fertility popped into my head. I knew the benefits of practicing yoga, and I was aware that since getting back on to my own mat, I was already seeing these benefits within my own body, mind and spirit. I did what most people do when they want to know something, and so I Googled it. Not only did I find a training specifically for yoga and fertility, but during my studies, I learned so much more than I ever thought I would. This training was beneficial for my own health and I knew what I was learning was worth sharing. It was after I completed this training that I decided I wanted to be more actively involved in the birth world. I invested in another program with my coach and another yoga training.

This story continues much the same now. I continue to invest in myself both personally and professionally. Becoming a mother has helped me identify where I hold on to trauma from childhood and my teen years, especially around my body. When my daughter triggers me, I know now there is something deeper I need to work through. I have become aware of how strong words can impact a person and I work hard to maintain my awareness so I don't add to other people's suffering. I continue to work with my coach and I continue to learn about fertility and how I can best support women so they feel the way they want to feel. I continue to learn about women's struggles and use it as fuel to keep sharing and putting myself out there. I continue to practice gratitude, and working through the limiting beliefs. Each time I put clothes on and look at myself in the mirror and feel that Incredible Hulk version of Maggie creeping up, I work even harder to shut that bitch down. Every day is a new day to learn and grow, and it has honestly changed my life in such a positive way. It's not easy, but the rewards are worth it. I feel lighter, I feel like I'm finally working with my body after a lifetime of working against it. I feel like I am now in a position to share my experiences with love and kindness because I have learned to love and be kind to myself. Every day I get a chance to show up and be the woman I want to be, and I am grateful for that. I'm grateful that I can do this work now. I'm grateful that one day, my daughter is going to look in the mirror and all she's going to feel is beautiful.

KEY TAKEAWAY

Maggie Callaghan

@femme.fertility
@momfidentaf
#selfloveclub

CHAPTER THREE

Marie Miller

Marie is an entrepreneur, self-discovery advocate, writer, and mama. She lives in a tiny hamlet in Northumberland County, Ontario with her husband and toddler. After spending over a decade feebly trying to climb the corporate ladder, Marie decided to throw caution to the wind and build her dream life. In a span of six weeks, she got married, bought a house, and had her daughter. Since then, she's been charging ahead with big plans and lofty goals. In 2020, Marie and her husband launched a small-batch, artisanal cultured butter company called Lofty Butter Company, where she affectionately identifies herself as the Chief Butter Officer. She dreams of a world that is filled with love and acceptance. In the meantime, she navigates her own self-love journey in a way that she feels is making a difference, starting at home as she models it for her daughter.

Find Marie:
@radiantselfcollective

I want to take you back to a specific moment in time: the moment that began my decades-long struggle with self-esteem challenges based on some very small things. These tiny little things added up to something way bigger.

My story is all about body hair.

Picture an eight-year-old girl who loved playing sports,who impressed others with her rap music knowledge (because she had an older sibling), and who enjoyed matching her socks to her outfits. On this particular day, she probably had on folded-down purple socks, with purple cotton shorts, and a Northern Reflections shirt adorned with cartoon mice and purple flowers. Maybe she even had a purple scrunchie in her hair. Purple, pink, teal – her outfit could've been any colour. The one thing that I'm sure of, though, is that she was wearing those cotton shorts

That day at school, this little girl was on the playground during recess – a time that had been one of her favourite parts of the day. Soccer, three-pitch, tag on the climbers, four-square – her little legs were on always on the move.

But I guess on that day, they weren't moving fast enough.

During recess, a boy at school focused a little too hard on

those legs of hers. This young girl had never had a fleeting bad thought about her legs. Or her body. Or her body hair, for that matter. She never felt that there was anything that made her "different" from the others. But that day she was on the receiving end of the first criticism of her body based on our hairless societal standards.

This boy pointed out that *GASP* her legs were covered in hair!

The summer's sun had done its work on turning her typical brown hair a golden hue of blonde, but that didn't matter. Hair was hair, and hair was there. Apparently, it was longer than his. And there was more of it on her legs than he had ever seen before. He felt the need to share this with her, at length, and ask around for support of his observation from their classmates.

Yup, it was confirmed: they were the hairiest legs anyone had ever seen.

And for the first time ever, she felt shame about her body and the hair that decorated its surface. That night, she went home from school and cried. She told her mom that kids had pointed out her leg hair and made fun of how much there was and asked why her legs were so hairy. At eight years old, this little girl returned to school the next day the same, but different.

This little girl was a new person. A girl who had felt judgement. A girl who reacted to the criticism and tried to "fix" herself. A girl that was told that hairy was not beautiful – not normal. She was now a girl with hairless legs, fighting against the new norm of never-ending stubble, razor nicks, ingrown hairs, and dry skin.

But, hey, at least her legs were smooth.

In grade 2, I began the difficult, time-sucking, self-esteem crippling, and society conforming journey of removing any evidence that my perfectly normal and human legs had hair on them.

At eight years old, I began shaving my legs.

I wish I could say that this was the end of my battle against my body hair – but of course, that wouldn't be much of a chapter. So, let me take you on a journey of the life of the hairy girl, and tell you how she finally found a way to love herself, hair and all.

Years passed, and along with countless hours of sports, homework, backyard explorations, and sleepovers, a great many hours were spent getting rid of my leg hair. By the time I was in grade four, I had tried so many things. I started with using my mom's electric razor. I'd hide away in the bathroom, armed with a white Braun electric razor and a container of baby powder. It hadn't taken long for me to learn that the dry razor had a tendency to pull at my tiny hairs. The carcinogen-laden talc powder helped it glide more smoothly as the oscillating blades worked their magic.

I moved on to other experiments: hair removal creams that literally burned my hair off at the follicles, at-home wax strips to try to rip the hairs out, cheap disposables, more expensive disposables, and finally, I was gifted my very own

Gillette SensorExcel. With its higher quality blades, sturdy and wide handle, and translucent blue wave pattern grip, it was a gift given out of love, but ultimately perpetuated my self-hatred.

I got into the groove of shaving my legs. They'd get prickly, and I'd deal with them.

My best friend at the time told me that she wasn't going to shave until she was 13. Her mom had told her that if you waited to shave, your hair would naturally fall out so that you wouldn't have to at all. She said that those who shaved early would have to spend their lifetime shaving because it would just keep getting thicker and grow back quicker.

I didn't believe her. But then, something happened.

A dark hair sprouted somewhere that there was never any hair before.

Think of the shock and horror that I felt when I noticed my first pubic hair growing. I was appalled. I was disgusted. I was terrified that I was becoming a hair-covered circus act. So I did what any scared 11-year-old child would do given the circumstances.

I shaved it.

This didn't last very long. Soon, I was dealing with painful infected bumps. For some reason, I didn't put two and two together and finally, with shame and fear, I asked my mom to look and see what was wrong with me. After a quick inspection, she told me I was fine; that it just looked like an ingrown hair.

I finally accepted that I couldn't keep shaving there. But in my innocent mind, I figured it would be okay. Nobody else would ever know because I would keep it hidden forever. I stopped changing in front of my friends. I started wearing shorts when I went swimming.

As long as nobody saw it, I was the same as them.

You'd think that battle would end there, but no.

In grade six, a boy in my class pointed out that I had a unibrow. I was comforted by being told that he was teasing me because, obviously, that meant he had a crush on me. You know the old adage, "Boys will be boys." This is a topic for another day, but despite the reasoning for why he said what he did, that comment led me to change something else about my appearance.

I began to regularly visit the salon. They would use hot wax, a popsicle stick, and cotton strips to rip my hairs out and shape my eyebrows. Thank God for the soothing aloe vera lotion they applied when they were done. I was told a countless number of times how beautiful my eyebrows looked, once they were "dealt with".

It was around this time that I also began to exhibit trichotillomania-type behaviours. Also called "hair-pulling disorder" this type of obsessive-compulsive disorder is where someone cannot stop pulling at or pulling out their hair.

During times of emotional distress or anxiety, I would find myself uncontrollably plucking my eyebrows. They would end up pencil-thin, or almost gone, and it essentially became a running joke. How stressed is Marie? Just take a look at her eyebrows and they'll tell you the story.

I pretty much had to have my tweezers and manicure scissors taken away from me, but that didn't stop the symptoms from showing up. I would pull on my eyebrows and the hairs on my head with my fingers until they came out.

Whether this is directly the result of my early experiences with body hair shaming, my anxiety, stress, genetics, or a combination them all, it has added another layer of complexity to my body hair story. Not only was I hairy, but I also had a weird impulse to pull my hair out - something that I had never heard anyone talk about.

This is something that I still deal with today. Although I have become much more mindful and recognize when I am pulling at my hairs a lot, I still do it. The symptoms show up, especially in times of high-emotion, stress, and anxiety (here's lookin' at you, postpartum), but I have gotten better at navigating those triggering emotions. Dealing with the emotions helps me mitigate the hair-pulling. And I also know not to tweeze my eyebrows when I'm feeling overwhelmed or emotional.

In grade nine, I dated a boy who was obsessed with porn. And although he never saw me naked, he told me that he liked it better when girls were "bare." We all know what he was talking about. So, for nine months, despite being hidden away under layers of clothes, I sought acceptance of my body by shaving again.

It was painful. It was itchy. And it was definitely not worth it. After that, I decided (once again) that I was never going to do that. By this time, I was well aware that pubic hair was normal (although not accepted by society for women to have), and that whoever chose to love me would also have to love that part of my body the way it is, naturally.

I wasn't successful at keeping this promise to myself. The demands of society can be crushing at times. By my early 20s, I had a regular hair maintenance routine: shave, often; wax eyebrows, at least once a month; trim the bush, when it got unruly. I also found a boyfriend that seemed to accept my body and my stance on body hair for what it was. Almost in the same breath, he also expressed the sentiment that I heard from every other boy I had dated. "I don't mind that you don't shave down there, but prefer it to be smooth." Ugh.

I cannot wrap my head around how entitled men (especially) feel about women's bodies. I had never, ever made a comment about a partner's appearance, especially regarding body hair, because I knew how hurtful it was. And I knew it wasn't my place to criticize the body of someone that I love. But after months of him not shaving his patchy, scraggly-haired face, I finally came out and said it. "When are you going to shave your face?"

His response: "When are you going to shave yours?"

The breath caught in my throat.

I had noticed over the past few years that the peach-fuzz on my face was going into unchartered territories of no longer being peach-fuzz. But I didn't think anyone else (except for my aesthetician who waxed my brows and had started asking if I wanted my chin done) had noticed. I never commented on anyone else's body hair again after that.

In my early 20s, I also started getting grey hairs. Great, something else to be embarrassed about, because, of course, only men are typically granted "silver fox" status. Promptly, I began colouring my hair.

Shave, trim, wax, cut, colour, perfect.

Fast-forward to another boyfriend, this one from my mid-twenties. He was from a culture that was repulsed by body hair. The women threaded or waxed everything but their heads and eyebrows, the men shaved their chests and armpits. He wanted me to be cleanly waxed from nose to toes. He would make comments about the body hair on other women, "The light hit her face and all I could see was her bleached moustache. It was so disgusting." And, of course, he commented about my body hair, too. "When are you going to shave?" "Would you consider waxing your arms?" "You should go get your legs done."

In addition to hairless bodies, there was the desire for me to have long flowing hair. So, any trim that seemed to go a little too far was met with criticism. "Why did you cut your hair so much? I like it better long."

Needless to say, it was post this relationship that I

really began to explore the damaging impacts of other people's opinions as it related to my self-esteem and self-worth. When I left that relationship, I cut all of my hair off, and dyed it all kinds of fiery reds, oranges, and yellows. I wanted to feel as though I owned my own body. I was tired of being controlled. I was tired of society telling me I wasn't enough. It felt good to take back control. I was finally starting to shake this need to conform, despite hearing the same rhetoric: you should grow your hair out, I don't like red hair, you should go get your eyebrows done, is it time for a bikini wax?

One would think that criticisms about another person's body would be reserved for being just from their enemies. But I've heard these comments from all types: friends, family, boyfriends, bullies, strangers. And as if it isn't enough hearing these things from all of these people, what society views as beautiful is reflected in all forms of media.

Magazines, movies, television shows, music videos, billboards, book illustrations, video games…From a young age, I was bombarded with the image of the perfect female body. The image of a thin, long-haired, large-breasted, tanned-skin, hairless body. There were razor ads in my Teen Vogue and on TV. Women never had grey hair. They didn't have armpit hair, nipple hair, or a bad hair day. And if they did? My, oh my, would the tabloids ever jump on that story!

I think about the hours I've wasted trying to hide my body, change my body, and have my body accepted by others. It wasn't until I had a daughter that I finally decided that this body is MINE. It does not exist to live up to anyone else's standards of beauty. It does not have to be bare to be beautiful. It does not need approval by my husband, my friends, strangers, or society.

A lot has changed in my life since those early days of navigating hair removal. I no longer get my eyebrows waxed on a regular basis. I am no longer afraid to wear a swimsuit because my bikini line isn't shaved. I am no longer afraid to go months without shaving at all.

I have also decided to embrace the fact that I have grey hair. At this point, all of the previous dye treatments have been cut away and I am left with my natural mane – dark brown with many flecks of white and sparkling silver. When I look at my hair, I feel like it has been a long coming-of-age journey, but that I am finally almost there. I am proud to have earned each one of these grey hairs, and to have grown to be old enough to have them all. I am okay that I am getting older, that my skin sags a bit more, my eyes wrinkle when I smile, and that I have a new found confidence to walk on this earth in this body – in MY body. I accept the fact that my body has hair. Everybody has hair. I have hair under my arms, and on my legs. I have hair on my back and my chest. I have hair on my face, on my stomach, and on my toes.

I have 5 million tiny reasons that I could hate myself.

But I've decided to show my daughter that beauty is not all about how bare you are.

Sometimes I go months without shaving because I feel empowered knowing that it no longer controls me and defines me. Sometimes I shave weekly because I want to. And sometimes, I sit in the car and pluck my chin hairs out because the lighting is perfect. The thing is, I am finally doing it because it is MY choice, not because I feel that I have to in order to be loved.

When my daughter was just 18 months old, she was playing with a relative when I heard them exclaim, "Feel those hairy legs!" My heart went into my throat. I yelled out, "Don't ever comment on her leg hair again!" I know that challenging societal norms will not change the world. I know that the world can be a cruel place and that it will take a lot of time and resistance among the masses to actually change society's perception of what is beautiful and what is acceptable. But this mama is going to keep speaking love into her little child. I don't know what I'm going to do if (and when) my daughter comes home, tears streaming down her face as she tells me that someone criticized her body. I don't know what I'm going to do if people make fun of her leg hair or her unibrow.

Will I be able to look at that little girl and tell her to ignore the comments and embrace herself for who she is? Or will her heartbreak make me want to help her navigate the world of conformity? Will I help her make the decision on how much she wants to change her body's appearance to appease the opinions of others? I don't have the answers, and I don't know if I will ever need to. But I do know that each day, I am going to tell my baby how beautiful she is. I am going to teach her to be kind to others. I am going to show respect to others by not commenting on their appearance, especially in their absence and in a negative way. I am going to spend each day not only loving her, but just as importantly, loving myself.

In a society that has made their opinion very clear – that body hair is ugly and something to be ashamed of, I am here to say that you are beautiful, and there's more than 5 million tiny reasons why.

KEY TAKEAWAY

Marie Miller

@radiantselfcollective
@momfidentaf
#selfloveclub

CHAPTER FOUR

Sanaa Geneski

Sanaa Geneski is a mother of three, wife and currently working as a Senior Financial Advisor with a large financial institution. Originally an Ottawa native, she has been residing in Ajax, Ontario for the last ten years. She enjoys writing, interior design and practicing Reiki, and can most often be found planning a party. Sanaa is working towards starting her own business that will incorporate her passion of energy healing, self-love coaching, and financial coaching.

Find Sanaa:
@hey.sanaa or email sanaageneski@gmail.com
Author Photo: Aaron Brown Photography

INSIDE-OUT

I want you to stand in front of your mirror. Naked. For real - do it today. I dare you to love yourself so hard, because you are beautiful. Every inch and every curve of you. Every stretch mark and every vein. I know that there are so many women out there that don't take the time to appreciate their own body because I was one of them. Would you believe it if I told you that I never once looked at myself naked until I was in my 30s? I would run out of the shower with a towel on and get my clothes on so that I didn't have to see myself.

I grew up in a culture where, in general, women are criticized about their bodies so blatantly and habitually that we become numb to it. Women's bodies are held to a much higher standard where I come from. Come to think of it, I tend to place the blame on my culture, when in reality all cultures need to do much better to eliminate body shaming. I was criticized so much growing up that my own self-talk became borderline abusive, which is terribly unfair and completely unacceptable. It starts with the people around us lying to us, telling us we are unworthy by criticizing how we look, suggesting that the way we look is not good enough, and then we subconsciously start doing it to ourselves. Even when we are not hearing it from society, we were never preconditioned to accept that human bodies come in all shapes and sizes and that no two bodies are equal.

I'm not suggesting that we can just decide to love our bodies and that is the end all and be all. Loving my body hasn't even been a priority of mine until recently. I've been working within myself for the last two years and only now am I starting to also work on the outside. How we look does not dictate our capabilities as humans, yet we've been conditioned to believe that who we are on the outside has to be who we are on the inside. If we don't fit into a cultural and societal standard of beauty, we are overlooked and deemed invaluable (...and as we all know as of late, social media has perpetuated this pandemic). I want you to appreciate your body, even for a brief moment, because regardless of what it looks like on the outside, it has provided a home for you. It has gotten you to where you are today and for that, every human that walks this earth should be grateful. By reflecting on my body and how it has served me in this life, I started to gain a sense of gratitude. In a span of 10 years, my body has endured five surgeries, four pregnancies, an abortion, weight gain, weight loss as well as nips and tucks! I've had scar tissue burned, an organ removed, a cyst sculpted out, two biopsies and three births in a four-year time frame. It allowed me to wake up for nursing and feed my babies. I was able to get myself to and from Ottawa so I could be with my dying mother. I can swim with my kids, go for hikes, I can move. My body is capable of a million things and yet the number one focus I have put on it is that I'm fat. How heartbreaking. What I say to you now is: Are you aware of how magnificent your body truly can be? Do you know how capable you are of loving yourself? Take the time to stop and admire just how beautiful of a being you are. You are so worthy.

EXPECTING THE UNEXPECTED

The last ten years of my life have been moving at a rapid pace. When I was 23, my doctor told me that I may have difficulty conceiving because I had just been diagnosed with endometriosis. I've always wanted a family, so when I was taking a pregnancy test at 26, not yet ready to be a mother, I was still hoping that the results were positive because I just wanted to be able to get pregnant. I welcomed motherhood with postpartum depression. Six weeks after birth, my husband and I conceived again. This time, a positive test result wasn't welcomed. Feeling like I had no control over my body, I decided to do something I never thought I would do. I had an abortion. I was left feeling scared and ungrateful. I told myself that because I made this choice, I was unworthy of grieving this terrible loss I had experienced. I wasn't equipped to take on the side effects of how traumatic it would be not only physically, but especially mentally. I resorted to suppressing my feelings, something I had been conditioned to do since adolescence. I didn't share my experience with anyone other than my husband and mother, for fear of being judged. I carried on with life and conceived my second child. Three pregnancies in one year was overwhelming. That was the first time I felt the need to better my life and do something positive for my health. I decided that after delivering, I would work hard to transform my body.

I spent my entire adulthood being overweight and I no longer wanted to be unhealthy. Since I'm being honest, I also wanted to conform to societal norms of beauty. I took control and worked hard to do something for myself. At the time, I thought working on myself physically was the only option for better health. I wasn't aware that my transformation needed to be from within. Nonetheless, I was doing well. I had two babies under two, I was advancing my career, I was focusing on physical fitness and health, and I was happy for a brief moment in time. It was then that my mother was diagnosed with cervical cancer. Hearing that diagnosis was completely shocking. Even though cancer diagnosis rates are sky-rocketing to one in two Canadians, I still never thought it would actually happen to my own mother. My mother and I had always been really close. I felt so helpless. I didn't know how I was going to maintain my new lifestyle while trying my hardest not to break-down emotionally. I couldn't quit motherhood, and I couldn't quit work, so I quit working out in order to focus on everything else. Shortly after, I was pregnant with my third child.

SURVIVAL

The first year of my mother's illness was manageable. She underwent a round of light chemo and radiation. Doctors were hopeful. I was pregnant and had two young children, so travelling back and forth to Ottawa was quite challenging. During that time, I just kept trying to maintain a positive mindset. Shortly after delivering my third, doctors discovered that the cancer had spread and it was now in her lymph nodes. They went on to say that it was terminal and she was given six to twelve months to live. At this point, I had three children under four. I was travelling back and forth to Ottawa to be with my dying mother and I was relying on my husband and mother-in-law to raise my kids while I was away. I was constantly riddled with guilt. No matter where I chose to be, I was deciding to be away from the ones I loved most. No matter how hard life was at the time, I still wasn't giving in to the pain. I kept going and kept myself distracted, so I wouldn't have to feel the sadness. I was told by everyone around me that I was so strong. I didn't cry much. I resorted to laughter over tears and I kept my composure. I wanted to be that strong person that everyone said I was. I liked hearing it and it gave me a sense of pride, a feeling I wasn't ever familiar with.

By the time my one-year maternity leave was over, I went back to work for one week when my mother was admitted to hospital for the last time. Taking a leave of absence from work and being there was a no-brainer. Now that I'm thinking back to that time, trying to put the words together, it feels heavy. I just want to go back in time give myself a hug because I know now that the months to follow were going to be excruciating. She was deteriorating at a rapid pace and watching it happen in real time was traumatizing. I kept telling myself that so many people before me had lost their loved ones and they survived it, so I could too. I've learned that as humans, we try and make our experiences relatable to other people's experiences. What I know now, is that every single experience is unique to the individual. I saw people around me that were living happy, healthy lives after they have lost a parent, spouse or sibling and thought, I too am capable. What I didn't see was their pain, their process, and the time it took to get to where they were. I was just looking at the end result and it distracted me from the present.

IT'S A PROCESS

The inevitable happened, and my mother passed away

It was a sunny July day.

Right before it happened, I'd taken a break outside of the hospital. I knew the end was near, but I didn't expect it so soon. I was laughing with one of my best friends. I remember how much we were laughing because it was refreshing. I wasn't even thinking about what was happening inside the hospital, and I was purposely taking my time to get back. When I did get back upstairs to her room, she was surrounded by my brother and my cousins. The energy in the hospital always seemed to be thick, but this time it was different. I knew something was off. Everyone just looked at me and said she was having a hard time breathing.

I took her hand in mine, and without even thinking about it, the words just came out: "Mom, it's okay, I'm here." In that moment, I watched her take her last breath. Ugh, it crushed my soul. That was it. The anticipation had been building up and I just kept trying to make it through the days but then she took her last breath, and there were no more days. All the built-up emotion came pouring out of me like a tap that had been backed up. I couldn't turn it off. I remember saying to my cousin: "How do you do it? I don't know how to do it." I was so concerned with staying strong and reassuring myself that I could survive a life without her, but I didn't know how the heck I was going to do it.

The next few days consisted of the funeral and sorting through her belongings. Then it was time to go back home. It was incredibly painful, however. I will admit I also felt a bit of relief. Relief that I no longer had to choose where I was going to be. No more back and forth, and no more guilt. The reality is that although I no longer had to choose, that guilt that I had built up for constantly having to choose, that didn't go away. I never addressed it, and by not dealing with it, it kept growing uncontrollably. Being away from my children for so long, and then working full-time made me feel like a bad mother. I didn't allow myself to grieve, because I felt like it would make me weak, and I enjoyed being told I was strong. It was the one thing I could hold onto and in some ways control, as my world had fallen apart. As much as I wanted to lock myself in my room, and be sad, I couldn't do it. On top of that, I felt an obligation to my employer and went back to work a week after my mother had passed. By not taking the time to heal, my mental health was drastically affected.

As time passed, the pain grew and I recognize now that what I was feeling was a strong sense of fear. I was terrified of being vulnerable because if I allowed myself to feel the pain, it might never go away. I became depressed, which I continued to suppress, and eventually I started to hate myself. My self-talk was so mean. I was constantly telling myself I was a bad mother. I didn't believe that I was doing well enough at work. I hated myself for all the things I thought I wasn't. Eventually, it caught up. Suppressing your feelings isn't sustainable and when you are in an excessive amount of pain, you become someone else. I hated who I was. I knew that I had to make drastic changes in my life and I finally gave in. When I allowed myself to give in to the pain and be vulnerable, is when I finally felt like the strong person I wanted to be. I allowed myself to cry. Something so simple and ordinary started my healing. I've now figured out that grief is not a process designed to harm us. It is a process that is designed to assist us in our healing and ultimately, our growth. I've learned that there is no right or wrong way to grieve. People around you will have their opinions, as they always do, but regardless, don't allow yourself to take on someone else's expectations of what your grieving process should look like. You move at your own pace, and you do what is best for you.

GROWING IS (R)EVOLUTION

For me, grieving is still an on-going process. I still have my moments where I just randomly need to release the tears. I could be driving, or cooking, or writing and my tears start flowing. I allow them to flow. I allow myself to feel. I do not suppress what I cannot control. I also allow myself to be happy. I think of how far I've come in this process and I can smile. After my mom passed, I wrote a note to myself on my mirror: "Don't allow her suffering to go to waste." I didn't want her to just die and let that be it. I wanted my life to be better because of it. Somehow, I knew that I had to be accountable to myself. I could no longer be accountable to anyone else if I wanted to feel better. I did not want my life to be heavy and dark. I wanted peace. I wanted to be a person my kids could be proud of. I just didn't know where to start.

I was scrolling on Instagram one day and I found Diana Eskander, a Love coach from Montreal. Her page said she was helping women find lasting relationships. I contacted her and said that I don't need help finding a relationship. I was already in a marriage. What I needed was to have a relationship with myself and I needed help loving myself, because I don't know how to. Talk about vulnerability! I called up a stranger and admitted something that I had never even said to myself, yet. We worked together via telephone calls and during that time, I had a big 'ol Oprah style a-ha moment. I was able to pinpoint that the self-hate I was inflicting on myself came from the fact that since my mother had passed, I believed that I no longer had someone to offer me unconditional love. I relied on my mother to forgive me for my mistakes and accept me as I am. She was always there for me and never judged. Diana asked me if I would speak to my daughter the way I was speaking to myself. Whoa, that was gut-wrenching. I would absolutely never speak to anyone the way I was speaking to myself, let alone my daughter. That was such a pivotal moment for me in my healing and it was then that I started to make positive changes in my life.

NURTURING POSITIVE SELF-TALK

Great changes do not just miraculously happen overnight. This has been a very long and slow growth process. Baby steps. It really took off when Diana encouraged me to start writing. I thought, what better way to start writing about self-love than with a love letter. After years of self-abuse, I was scared to take that first step of showing love to myself, so instead, I wrote my first letter to my daughter:

"Dear Elsie,

You are going to make mistakes. You are going to break hearts. You are going to get your heart broken. No matter what, you are still worthy of love, you are still worthy of happiness, you are still worthy of a chance to change."

That was the truth I so badly needed to hear. When I read it back to myself, I felt like I had just taken a gasp of fresh air. I repeated to myself that I may be going through a very difficult season of life right now, but I am worthy of happiness. I may not be the best version of myself right now, regardless, I am still worthy of a chance to change. I continued on in my journey. It was still very difficult but I made small changes in the way I would speak to myself. I think we are all guilty of self-criticism, but I try and be mindful of the little things. When I catch myself saying, "I'm such an idiot" when I make a mistake, I pause, reflect on what just happened and correct myself. This is where the positive self-talks comes in and holds so much weight. I tell myself, "No, you're not an idiot. We all make mistakes. Just be more mindful of what you are doing."

BABY STEPS AND BIGGER THINGS

Those little moments that we often ignore, have made it easier for me to be kinder to myself when the bigger things happen. While I worked on my self-talk, I also started to incorporate more self-love "rituals" as I like to call them. Six months after my mother had passed away, I saw a medium. She recommended that I take up Reiki[2].

---

2 Reiki is a Japanese therapy technique to promote healing and reduce stress. It is believed that we have seven main points of energy in our bodies and over time and with trauma, these energy centres become blocked. When your chakras are blocked, your energy vibrates at a very low level, making you more prone to stress and illness. A Reiki practitioner gently moves their hands around the body, activating the relaxation response and works to unblock the chakras and help the body re-balance itself. As your chakras become unblocked, you vibrate at a much higher level and you become happier and healthier, hence the phrase "good vibes only".

I didn't do as she suggested and take up Reiki right away; I think maybe I just wasn't ready to dig into something new. When the time came, however, the universe made it very clear to me. My ever so pesky inner-voice kept telling me I needed to get back to Reiki. (By now you're probably thinking: geez, does her inner-voice ever stop talking?!) The simple answer is no! I don't imagine anyone can shut the inner chatter off. I then met a wonderful woman by the name of Conny Fisher, a friend of a colleague who also happened to be a Reiki practitioner. I know that this is going to sound so far-fetched, but I truly believe that my mother sent her to me. Whenever I am with Conny, I feel so connected to my mother's spirit, it's indescribable. I committed to a Reiki schedule, and the magic of healing started to take place.

When I first started my Reiki sessions, it was a nice way to physically relax and relieve stress. As time went on, I started feeling a deeper level of healing. Traumas from my past started coming to the surface. Events dating all the way back to my childhood were brought back to my consciousness and I realized it was because they were unresolved. Reiki really helped me connect with myself on an unprecedented level and it was only then that my true healing manifested.

By re-living these traumatic moments in my life, it became easier to be kinder to myself and gentler with my healing. Instead of hiding my true self, I am able to share and get a deeper sense of who I am. I believe we are all just spiritual beings having a human experience and what happens to us as children and throughout our lives shapes who we are. Some of it has a positive outcome, while the rest, not so much. It is completely up to us to initiate our healing and stop the habits that have been passed on to us from generations of pain. I can confidently say that Reiki has completely changed my life for the better. It has introduced me to a life of meditation, gratitude and abundance.

BUTTERFLY

My mother loved butterflies. I made a promise to her on her deathbed: I promised that every time I would see a butterfly, I would think of her. My favourite time of the year is now that time when spring rolls around and I spot my first butterfly. Partly because I smile and think of my mother, but it's also because butterflies are now a representation of who I've become. The dissolving of my past self, the messy goo of a life I had to evolve through and the cocoon made up of the burdens that I wrapped myself up in. By taking this journey of self-love, I now see myself not just as "a mother, a wife, plus so much more," I see myself as an individual worthy of love. I am free to be myself because I am working hard to be the best version of myself. That mental shift in how I love myself and view myself has benefited how I view those that I love most. I am so much more confident as a mother now.

I adore my husband and my children, but just as I am my own individual, so are they. I will never take that away from them and I don't feel the need to impose my idea of what their life needs to be (like a lot of our parents did to us). By loving myself, and treating myself with kindness, we are all growing in an environment created in love. An environment where I am working hard to eliminate judgment and fear. They will learn to make personal growth a priority, because I am able to lead by example. Kindness to ourselves will pour out onto those around us. My family will be compassionate to themselves and to others because I will be compassionate with myself and with them. I will be vulnerable with my children and teach them to be vulnerable with themselves. As my children grow, all I want is that they feel seen, heard, and loved. I am able to provide a safe environment for that to take place, because I am creating that within myself. My biggest fear has always been that my mistakes will define who I am. My greatest accomplishment to date is that I've proven to myself that I can be accountable for my mistakes and learn from them. My relationships can only get better from here.

AWAKENING - TOOLS FOR CONTINUAL GROWTH

Like everything, positive changes in our lives take practice and understanding. If something requires practice, then failure is inevitable. By pushing aside the fear of failure, we can introduce new practices in our lives that can further our growth. Meditation is a wonderful place to start. What I love about meditation is that it is completely non-judgemental. It is a personal practice that has no weight or measurement of success, so even if we don't get it right the first few times, absolutely no one will know and we can keep trying.

There are many resources or apps to assist with taking on this practice and every single beginners' guide will teach you to start slow and at your own pace. Our lives are so full of all the things we need to accomplish at work, at home, for our children, our partners and everything in between. By practicing meditation regularly, you can take a few minutes a day that belong to only you. The focus is to stay present in your breathing and forget everything else that is going on. What this practice has taught me is that in the moments in my busy life, when my mind wanders aimlessly, I am able to recognize it, and bring my focus back to the present moment. When we are living in the present, there is no longer room for worrying about what might possibly go wrong next, or even dwell on what has happened in the past. That is the root of anxiety and depression. I know that your life is so busy; all our lives are. Fill those moments in-between the chaos and do something small that is just for you.

In addition to meditation, I mentioned gratitude and abundance. Those two go hand in hand. I remember when my love coach first mentioned the word "abundance". I was slightly embarrassed because I didn't know what it meant. There is the dictionary definition meaning a very large quantity of something, and then there is the spiritual definition. Spiritually, an abundant life refers to a sense of satisfaction with what we already have, regardless of the material objects we own. I didn't know how to achieve that, but I knew I really wanted it. We all have a lot to be grateful for, but we find ourselves wanting more.

Social media makes it difficult to keep up with everyone around us. People are constantly sharing the best part of their lives and themselves, leaving out the messy parts. The travels, the wedding, the babies – just what society views as positive accomplishments. Subconsciously, we have to battle with these imaginary lifestyles and it makes it difficult to appreciate what we actually have. Having goals and ambitions in life are great. It keeps us evolving as humans. There isn't anything wrong with wanting more, but if we don't stop to appreciate what we have now, nothing will ever be enough. The path to abundance starts with the practice of gratitude.

One way to practice gratitude is to keep a journal. Day by day, start writing what you are grateful for. I can promise you that it's going to start off with the basics: I'm grateful for my life, my husband, my kids, a roof over my head, I have food, clothes, a job, a car... etc. We have access to clean water, healthcare and we are fortunate to live in a society where poverty and corruption are less rampant than anywhere else in the world. It is okay to be grateful for these things, but when practicing daily gratitude, eventually you run out of the obvious answers and then you start looking for more things to be grateful for. When we start expressing gratitude to the tiny moments in life that were previously overlooked, we are able to develop a love for life that we have.

RETROSPECTIVE

I was once told that I shouldn't share my pain with people because nobody cares. I believed it, and it hurt. I had emotional pain and trauma that I had been carrying around most of my life. It's a part of who I am. A large source of that pain came from the idea that I was alone in my circumstances. If only someone in my family, or in my social circle had just shared with me that they too, have pain, it would have eliminated the isolation I had created in my mind. So, yes, there will be people who don't care. People who don't want to read my posts, or my story. So-*damn*-what! I won't let that stop me from sharing my truth. My truth is what lead me to this journey of self-love. I know for certain that at least one person will benefit from me opening up and being vulnerable.

I was in your place before, looking for a way out. Looking for someone to help me love myself. We are all humans just trying to figure this life out for the first time and it can be difficult and daunting. If we support each other, we can work together to eliminate the preconceived societal notion that we are selfish if we love ourselves. For that, I will take on the discomfort of sharing my pain and help give that one person hope that happiness is a real possibility.

I want you to know that you are capable, you are worthy, and you have a lot to offer this world. Take control of your happiness and watch as you bloom into the best version of yourself. Don't be scared to take up space; that is what you were born to do. Put your growth first and watch everything in your life fall into place.

I'm proud to say that I really love who I've become. I still make mistakes and sometimes I hurt people I love, but I understand that there will always be things I need to work on. I'm never going to be the perfect mother, wife, or friend. I'm not in the pursuit of perfection, but instead, I'm committed to striving for continuous growth and perpetual self-love.

KEY TAKEAWAY

Sanaa Geneski

@hey.sanaa
@momfidentaf
#selfloveclub

CHAPTER FIVE

Shelley Taylor

Shelley is a strength based leader who lives to inspire through developing strengths while using her abundant energy and always having fun. Shelley has been a long time fitness enthusiast leading group fitness along with personally competing in running, swimming and cycling events. As a coffee master with Starbucks Coffee Canada, ST leads her district through her energy, not only from the coffee passion and knowledge she has acquired but also through her positivity. Shelley is a mother of 2 incredible teen aged humans and is married to a loving supportive husband and is the proud owner of 2 pups and a horse. As a constant learner, she continually grows and shares.

Learn, Share, Grow, B-STrong!

Find Shelley:
@ststrengths | www.ststrengths.com

Imposter. Fraud. This is me. Or at least that is what I felt at the beginning of writing this. Self-love is damn hard. What I have discovered on this journey, is that it is a journey. No end game. We are playing an infinite game. One that doesn't have a winner, a loser or even a tie. Wait, whaaat? No score? No rank? Quite a difficult concept to grasp coming from a competitive spirit. This is a concept that keeps evolving over time. One that morphs and teaches us random things at random times, through random acts and random humans. There is one HUMUNGOUS learning through self-love discovery where I find I get the biggest return on investment on loving harder and stronger. Shall I start with the punch line?

FAILURE. Perceived Failure. Struggle. Setbacks. Lessons. Whatever the heck you want to call it. I can graciously admit that I have fortunately lived a super easy and fulfilling life. I grew up with two loving parents who gave me and my one sibling a good life – food, an education, support, love and experiences. I didn't lose at much. Please let me explain. I don't want to come off as a pompous asshole[3] who is bragging about a life handed to me. I made most (not all, but most) of the sports teams I tried out for; I got most (not all, but most) of the jobs that I went after; I had and still do

3 Editor's note: "Shelley Taylor is most definitely not a pompous asshole. I can vouch for that." - Courtney St Croix

have a circle of incredible friends who connect with at least once per year without ever skipping a beat. I got good grades in school. I got into all the schools I applied for. I have my health and am continuously working on financial wealth. Although my life has been rewarding, one thing I know for sure is that I always put in the effort, and I say **YES**. Regularly. This is where my self-love strengthens and has grit. I have to say it over and over and over again. "I put in the effort and I say YES," therefore it is okay to love myself.

YES! That's it. [insert mind explosion emoji.] I am not an imposter. I am not a fraud at the self-love game. I EARN my self-love. It's not just handed to me. I earn the right to say I love myself. It's quite okay.

Let's go back to fourth grade. I believe this was a pivotal occurrence and where my self-love journey began. In a classroom with an incredible teacher who taught us things that were definitely not on the curriculum, like Morse code; who brought exotic pets into the classroom, and who taught us to think for ourselves. My fourth grade teacher shared vividly, one very valuable lesson: to say **"YES"**, before you can think to say no.

It was 1983, and I had just made the junior cross-country team. Without displaying a runner's physique and having never run further than to my friend's house on the court we grew up on, I made the team. Proud as ever, we went to our regional cross-county meet in Longwoods Conservation area. Competing on the Mitchell Elementary school team, our senior runners on that wet, rainy day were caught up in some eighth grade graduation prep work, which took them away from competing in the meet on that dreary day.

Our coach wanted representation in all age groups, so asked me to run in the grouping for seventh and eighth grade, instead of in the grouping of which I belonged: fourth to sixth grade. Without hesitation (and to be completely honest, without realization), I said **YES**. Why not? What's the worst that could happen? I come in last? The older, more mature and more developed kids alongside little scrawny me line up at the trees. The starter gun goes off and I immediately lag noticeably behind all the other kids who were three and four years older than me. As I am huffing and puffing with my grey jogging pants, blue three-striped sweatshirt and Dorothy Hamill haircut, I feel myself losing my breath, slipping in the muddy mess and I start to think…*why* did I say **YES**? What was I *thinking*? Trying my best to keep up, I fall down a steep hill, get grass and mud stains all over my trackers and persevere to cross the finish line after four kilometres. As I was approaching the finish line, with all the cheers from parents, fellow students and teachers, I hear from the announcer, "And congratulations to our last place runner – Shelley Ramsay!"

SNAP – a photographer captures the moment beautifully. Ugh. I came in dead last. The worst that could have happened, did in fact happen. Caked with dirt and tears rolling down my face, complete exhaustion taking over my body and total defeat, I got on the yellow school bus that took us back to our school so I could be completely embarrassed with my now ripped and filthy knees, drenched hair and clothing and red puffy eyes. I remember thinking to myself, *I will never say* ***YES*** *and do anything outside my age group ever again.*

Well, that particular "**YES**", even though it didn't provide me the outcome I expected, earned me an "Athlete of the Month" nod, and that muddy, last-place photo wound up in the local Mitchell Town Crier. This is a big deal when you are in the fourth grade! It gave me just enough of a confidence boost to love myself again and to say **YES** to a shit ton more things outside my age group!

It takes courage to say **YES**. It risks scrutiny and defeat. It challenges success. It forces the unknown. It perhaps makes you a beginner again. Since the fourth grade, I have said **YES** to endless activities without thinking. I would have not done so many wonderful things if I would have questioned any of my **YES** moments. (BTW, say "**YES**" with a fist and draw it quickly into your gut with an exaggerated sss at the end of it all.) I would have never tried out for and made the baseball team of two age groups older than me; I would have never made the field hockey team and played for the senior team in high school while in the tenth grade. I would have never gone to university at the age of 17 and lived in a house with two guys I didn't know. I would have never gone to that party where I met my boyfriend. I would have never been the youngest manager in a successful fitness company when I first started. I would have never moved to the big city of Toronto and married my husband who I met at that party I said **YES** to. I would have never run my first marathon or completed my first ½ Ironman. I would have never gone back to school and earned my Bachelor of Education. I would have never owned a cottage. I would have never taught group fitness or presented on stage at conferences. I would have never had two children; I would have never learned empathy. I would have never gone on wild and crazy "girl" trips or swam across a lake for kids. Without **YES**, I would have not discovered a whole new world of coffee and culture I never even knew existed. And of course… I would never have been co-authoring a book.

As I dug deeper and reflected on what saying **YES**, really, truly meant, I discovered it is just another form of focusing on and leaning in to your strengths. Strength discovery has been my passion since reading my very first Marcus Buckingham book: *Now, Discover your Strengths.* We all tend to believe that strengths are things that we are good at, and weaknesses are what we are bad at. In fact, strengths are things that "strengthen" us (that bring us joy) and weaknesses are things that we loathe; things that deplete us of our energy. We may be good at something but hate doing it. For example, I am good with numbers, and I understand math and accounting well. But you know what? That shit weakens me. To sit still and analyze numbers and balance spreadsheets even though I am pretty damn good at it, is a weakness. On the flip side, I suck at running. I am slow, I breathe heavy, I struggle, I sometimes need to stop and take a break. But I love it. It is a true strength of mine. I love every waking second of it. I look forward to it. I do not have the shape, the technique, the weight, the height… but, man, do I love it. Strength.

The love I have for "myself" comes from the love I have for what I do, choose to do, or choose not to do. I do say **YES** to stuff that gets me in big doo-doo, too. Have you ever said **YES** to too much, and you have trouble fitting it all in? Or, have you ever said **YES**, and then have to let it go or you just forget about it? That's where I get twitchy. I want to do it all, but it's so hard to be successful at that. There is no self compassion or love cultivating when you feel like you are overwhelmed, and those "imposterville" feelings set in.

I get easily embarrassed. (I'm working on it, but it still happens.) One of those embarrassing moments happened just a few short years ago. I had been with a company I believed in with all my heart, gave my love and passion and energy and soul to it, and identified with and truly was the only thing I knew and was known for. And then, one day: *POOF*, just like that, it was gone. To clarify, I had a choice to stay, take a pay cut and a demotion, and to that I chose to say **no**. Trust me, this was one of the hardest decisions I have ever had to make. Something tugged at me. I could choose to follow my strengths and move onward, or choose to stay comfortable with what I knew. I took the unknown path. I felt like an ultimate failure, that everyone would see. Without realizing it, I was getting a total hate on with myself. After job searching for a short time and getting either nowhere or being told no, I turned inward. I ran every day, started believing in my abilities, stopped depending on my former brand and started saying **YES** to everything crossing my path. Once I started saying **YES** again, the doors were opening. A few new opportunities presented themselves: a "kinda/sorta" job offering with a teaching organization overseas (totally in the strength zone); another job offering in the banking sector (remember, I am good at that, but it's definitely a weakness of mine as per my previous definition); and eventually landed my new role with a culture like no other and endless opportunities globally. I had to say **YES**. Utilize my strengths or develop them to say the least.

Since taking on this newfound role and working diligently through a very steep learning curve, I have gained weight, lost connections with people close to me, I travel a copious amount but I am learning (keyword: learning) to love myself more and more each day. Because I am following my strengths. Learning, sharing, growing and giving it my all. Every. Single. Day. Discovering what is possible and saying **YES** all day, every day.

Through this journey I would like to share my key learnings in self-love. I am no expert. I have experience. I am no guru, I have put in hours. I have short listed a few of what I know to be true, for your enjoyment:

1. Focus on your strengths.

These are the things that make you jump out of bed in the morning. The things that make time fly by. The things that make you late for that meeting. The things that you can stay up all night for, or get up really early for. Focus all your energy here and you will be lovin' thy self beyond measure. This will be a self-discovery of finding your true purpose. *My* purpose is to inspire through strength-based teaching and learning and be the first to do it while always having fun! What's yours?

2. Say YES to shit!

It's risky. It's rewarding. I love the age old saying: "Say, **'YES'**, then figure it out later." Most of my life has been this. I jump in, try, do, figure out and move on. No matter the outcome. This is livin'.

3. Say NO (to shit you hate)!

This is where it sounds contradictory. It's okay to say NO. Especially to the shit you hate. The energy sucking stuff. The stuff that doesn't build on your strengths. This is where finding your purpose helps. If it isn't fun, I isn't doin' it! (read that out loud in a twangy voice, okay?)

4. Be authentically vulnerable.

As Brene Brown says it best, "to be vulnerable means to show up and be seen. To ask for what you need. To talk about how you're feeling. To have hard conversations." This is where my give-a-shit meter has dropped as time goes by. If my intention is good, and I state my path, I truly cannot give a shit of what people say when I am not there.

5. Know when to stick with it, or when to quit.

This is the hardest skill for me, and am still practicing it regularly, but I know it is extremely true. I lived it. I chose it. I can swear by it. The word "quit" is harsh. I never believed it in. I always thought of it as negative. It means, by definition, to stop doing something. This is not bad thing at all. I stop eating when I am full. I stop talking when I listen. I stop doing things when they don't serve me or my purpose. Know when to quit. It's okay to do so if things don't feel right.

6. No more shadows.

Live your own beautiful, authentic life. Challenge the status quo. Be okay with having and sharing a different opinion. Stand out and stand up.

7. Wish and do. Wish again, and do, do, do.

We all have dreams and wishes. They can't come true without the *do*. Do something little each day to make it happen. Actions are way louder and more real than thoughts. It starts with just one chapter. You never know where it will go. Read. Read a lot. Apply. Apply a little. Learn. Learn a lot. Share a little of what your learned. Grow. Grow a lot.

8. Fail, because it's not a bad word ...and embrace the "blue sky"

This is the last of what I know to be true. Saved for the end and quite on purpose. Each time I have failed, whether it be for real (i.e., coming dead last in a race) or perceived (lost my role in an organization that I loved so much), it has taught me more than any success I ever had. I am not sure why. Perhaps, it's appreciation, gratitude, a sense of accomplishment, or self-reflection. I do know that I love myself more because of what I learned and conquered. I have been told many, many times that I have a "blue sky" over me, it follows me and that I need to see the other side or be "more real." Guess what? I am real. I do really see the good. I want to remain forever optimistic. It just feels good. It's who I am, and I shouldn't have to absorb pessimistic perspectives just because other people aren't eternal optimists, too.

This self-love thing is far from being mastered. There are days I stay in and choose to "not do" because I am not loving what I see, feel or think. But… (and is a BIG but), there are more days of saying heck **YES**. The **YES** that exposes and perhaps opens a world of opportunity or a chance at failure. A world where doors may just open. A world where my flaws will show. A world where my fourth grade self has no realization of what that **YES** means. A world where the give-a-shit meter sits at zero and the needle doesn't move. A world where this self-love game is infinite, ever evolving and holds true to its imperfections and road to excellence and not perfection. As I finish my chapter at the very last possible second, the hesitation to share my story at the beginning stemmed from the fact that I thought I didn't really have as story to share. It has just been a lot of saying **YES**, developing strengths, learning, sharing, growing, and carrying on. Let this self-love game go on no matter which way you look at it.

Thank you for allowing me to share what I know to be true. It may not be the same truth for you and that's okay. Thank you for allowing me to be my true authentic and easy going self. Thank you for reading the story that I didn't believe I had. Thank you for this incredible life that has one continuous blue sky that floats overhead.

May we all live our purpose and find our own self-love.

KEY TAKEAWAY

Shelley Taylor

@ststrengths
@momfidentaf
#selfloveclub

CHAPTER SIX

Katherine Burk

Katherine is a digital marketing entrepreneur who lives in Clarington, Ontario with her husband and young children. She is a former law-enforcement officer who took a leap from the life she knew, to live a life she could have only dreamt of. She is passionate about reading and writing and loves creating unique and effective content for her clients. She is proud of her budgeting knowledge and as a hobby loves helping people make their money work for them. When she doesn't have her head in a book she is chasing after her beautiful children and making memories to last a lifetime.

Find Katherine:
@bibsandbudgets | burkdigitalfactory.com

This life I live is nothing like the life I imagined for myself. The Katherine that you meet today is not the woman I thought I would be. It has taken a lot of love to understand that this is okay. Before I could truly love who and where I am today, I had to lose and grieve the life I thought I would be living. My journey to self-love has little to do with loving my body. Instead, I focus on the things I have accomplished, my failures and successes. Before living in the now, I was driven and sure of my path. I was a "go-getter" going after an ambitious career. Having two kids before thirty years of age was certainly not on my to-do list, (sorry, kids!) but life had other plans for me. Plans that I understand now, but at the time were devastating. My story isn't ground-breaking. I didn't overcome incredible feats, and I had immense support along the way. But if, like me, you have failed and felt like you were lost, you just might be able to relate. My story is all about loving yourself as you are now. Even if the you that you see today isn't the you that you had imagined you would be.

It all started in high school. Remember when you were fourteen and you were asked to figure out your whole life before you've hardly lived any of it? For me this question was easy, and it didn't take me long to decide that pursuing a career in law enforcement was the path for me. It was familiar; my father worked in corrections. I knew about the long hours, the shift work, and being away from family. I have always found the law interesting; add the excitement of police work and I knew this was right up my alley. I wanted to make my mark and make a difference for good. So, there it was, I had set my path and there was no going back.

I had always been driven. As a teenager, I fought competitively in Taekwondo. I was even lucky enough to compete for Canada in the Pan-Am Games. I knew what it was like to work hard and I had always gone after what I wanted. I wasn't always the best, but I worked hard. I was good at the sport and I enjoyed the success of being good at something. In general, things came easily to me. From my past experiences, I knew that if I put in the work, I would undoubtedly get the results I wanted. Though I had failed along the way, no failures were ever enough to knock me off my feet. I entered post secondary education knowing that I would certainly achieve my goal.

When I reflect on why I chose this career path, I don't have regrets. But I have come to find that part of my making this choice was a limiting belief. Though I overcame great obstacles in the pursuit of this path, I also felt like it was the only path I could do. I remember thinking that I wasn't smart enough for University, so how could I do anything else? Looking back, I wish I could have given myself a hug and told myself I truly could do anything I put my mind to. If any of your life decisions start with a "can't", I hope you can see past this. I wish I had been able to understand that I could do whatever I wanted. I may have chosen policing either way, but I wish I hadn't done so out of a belief that I couldn't do anything else.

I couldn't wait to start college. Hello, freedom to do whatever I wanted! Stay out late, have fun, meet new people. It really was one of the best times I've ever had. Though I certainly had lots of fun outside of the classroom, I was also inspired by learning. I was a good student and I was passionate about what I was learning. Traffic law, fingerprinting, analyzing evidence—it was all so cool and so interesting. I had finally found something I was good at!

Unlike other college programs, physical fitness was a requirement to graduate. Though I had once been an athlete, I struggled with weigh gain in my second semester. I nearly didn't pass my fitness classes. Though it wasn't easy, I persevered and did what it took to make my dreams a reality. This was not without struggle. There were many times that I felt as if I simply could not do it. Though I eventually succeeded I now believe this is where my self-doubt began to set in. The struggles I faced planted a seed that I wasn't the type of person who could pass this test. But life carried on, I made the cut and eventually graduated, but not without emotional baggage.

Despite my earlier doubts that I was smart enough, I graduated with honours. I was then able to transfer my credits towards a University Degree. At this point, I had already done more than I had ever believed I could. I had told myself I couldn't possibly be smart enough to go to University just a few short years before, and yet here I was. Not only did I attend, I graduated too. Once again, I had confirmed for myself that if I worked hard I could and would get what I had hoped for.

Like any recent graduate, I now found myself ready to take on the world. I quickly secured employment as a security guard at a major museum. Cool right? Within a year I landed another great job in my field as a Special Constable. I was so excited to have my dreams start taking shape and get moving on my career aspirations. Though I wasn't there yet, I was working at a great job, making good money, and gaining new skills and experience along the way. While I was working as a Special Constable, I was also working towards my end goal. I liked my job, but I still had to keep moving. I knew I still wanted to be a police officer of course. It was all coming together, and I could visualize my success. Yet, like anything that's sounding too good to be true, life threw me a few curve balls. Thankfully, these curve balls helped me build a life that I love, but I had to get through a lot of fog to see the light behind what happened next.

I was 23 years old, working in my industry while aggressively pursuing my other ultimate career goal. I was putting out applications, attending interviews, passing tests. Almost all my spare energy was used to do things that would help me get to where I thought I wanted to be. If you don't know about the police recruiting process, it's intense. I put my best foot forward and gave it my all and after all the success I had been riding on, I was sure to make the cut. Right? I had to. This was me after all. I played by the rules. I worked hard. There was no way I wouldn't make it. But behind all this something was bothering me. Something just didn't feel right, but I just didn't know what it was yet.

The feeling of something being "off" never left me. Though I was still going through the motions of interviewing and putting out applications, my heart was no longer in it. I can't pinpoint exactly what changed in me, but I can tell you that a lot of small (and some big) things happened while I was going through the motions. I If you haven't guessed already, I'm not a police officer. I don't even work in the field anymore. In the very last step of the interview process, I failed. It felt like a punch to the gut, even though I wasn't sure I even wanted it anymore.

After failing to do what I had once felt was my calling, I didn't know what to do. Couldn't I simply try again? Of course, I could. But in my disappointment, I retreated. How do you feel when everything you've ever worked for doesn't come to be? I know that I was hurt to my core. I was embarrassed and ashamed of myself. I tried to play it off like I didn't care, but you can be sure that I did. How do you not feel that you aren't good enough? How do you move past thinking that you simply aren't worthy? Maybe you won't be able to relate to my law enforcement path. But I bet you've gone for something before and had it not happen. You likely know what this hurt feels like, and it's really no fun at all.

Through everything that was going wrong there was also so much going right. Around the time that all of this was happening, I was also going through some really exciting life changes. My boyfriend, now husband, had proposed to me a few days before I started my first "real job" as a Campus Police Officer. Though I was dealing with so much stress and disappointment, I was also living in one of the happiest times of my entire life. We had a dream wedding just over a year later and quite soon after that we found out I was pregnant. This was a whole new layer to my life that truly changed everything. Though I had initially thought I would return to work after having our son, I couldn't shake my unexpected need to be home. I already knew that my career wasn't feeling like a good fit. I felt a lot of anxiety around going back. But it was more than that. I loved being with my family and we found a way to make that happen.

Like many families, slashing our income wasn't something to take lightly. But what the heck was I supposed to do now? All I thought I knew how to do was work in a field I no longer wanted anything to do with. Here's where some reinvention comes into play. We got creative, and I learned a new skill. I started teaching Chinese children English and here I was. Not "police" Katherine, but a work-at-home mom that sings with Chinese four-year old's every morning. It nearly makes me laugh out loud to think that this would be the path I would end up on. But I can't tell you how much I am glad that I'm here. I love what I do and I love being able to be present with my children, something I never felt would be possible in the past.

Picking up the pieces of the life I thought I would be living wasn't easy. I spent about a year unsure if I really wanted to move on or return to my "old life". I faced a lot of doubt and even considered applying to other jobs in the field along the way. Deep down, I knew that going back to the workplace wouldn't be the right call for me or my family. It was a big risk and I still wonder what my life would be like if I stayed. But the risk has been so worth the reward. I hope that when the time comes you trust yourself and take that big risk too.

You don't have to be the person you were. Whether that be the high school you, the you from a year ago, or even the you that you were yesterday. It sounds so simple. But this is something that has never been easy for me. As much as I knew that the life, I had planned for myself wasn't the one for me, I simply couldn't fathom how to move on. I am in a good place now but at the time I felt stuck. What would my co-workers think? What would my family think? What would the people from college, even high school think? I consistently found myself worried about what others would think about me.

I attached so much effort into my goal, it truly became my life. It even became a part of my personality, I lived and breathed what I wanted to be. I had always been Katherine, the one who wants to be a police officer. So, who would I be if I was no longer that person? I didn't know, and it scared me. I felt like an absolute failure. Yet, at the same time, I found an unexplainable sense of relief in the thought of distancing myself from her. I didn't want to be that Katherine anymore, though she is and will always be a part of me.

But how did I get over this fear of not being who I thought I was supposed to be, the person I told everyone I would be? Well, I'm not entirely sure what made me make a shift but small efforts over time shaped my reality. More important than anything else, I simply started living my life for me. I can't say I don't care what anyone else thinks of me, but it weighs on me much less. I am starting to understand that even if they do think about me, others likely think of me far less than I assume they do. Their thoughts are also likely nowhere near as critical as my own thoughts about myself. It's not that I don't matter to others, it's simply that they matter more to themselves than I do to them. I needed to matter more to myself than how I thought others felt about me. I started this internal conversation with myself with saying, "so what?"

So what if I didn't make it?

So what if I have completely changed paths?

So what if I have a degree in a field I don't work in?

So what if I have disappointed others along the way?

So what if I have changed?

So what if I'm not the person others remember?

So what if I've gained weight?

I braced myself with "so what's" as a sort of defence mechanism against my negative thoughts, my fears of what others would think of me. Though they served me for a time, I soon found that "so what" meant I was still living for other people's thoughts of me versus for myself. It still placed someone else's perceived opinion of me before my own opinion of myself. Letting go of all these thoughts was hard and I do still think about them at times. But I am learning that these conversations I have with myself can be framed in a much more positive light. My "so what's" showcase my insecurities. They are what I think to myself when I am trying to justify my actions to others. But there is no need for me to justify myself to anyone. "So what" is a step in the right direction, but "so what" still assumes that someone else is judging me. I now know that person was me.

Loving one's self is not something that always comes naturally, and it certainly didn't to me. More often than not, we are told to not love ourselves. We are told that we need to change. To look, feel or act in a certain way. Though this is what we are told, it's a lie. In order to love ourselves we need to let go of looking for approval of others and stop judging ourselves. The language we use to talk about or to ourselves can go a long way in making this shift.

In order to love who I am, I needed to start speaking to myself out of love. I needed to remove judgment from the equation. Others probably weren't judging me, but I certainly was judging myself. It's was a simple shift, but changing my "so what" into "what-ifs" made all the difference. My "what-ifs" highlight my strengths and not my insecurities. They place value on who I am as a person and remove judgment. "What-if" is a powerful shift. I would urge you to consider any time you've braced yourself with a "so what" and try to frame it into a "what if" statement.

What if I am happy?

What if I love the life I live?

What if I love being a mom?

What if I've found talents I never knew I had?

What if I love myself as I am?

What if I am capable of so much more than I have imagined?

What if I am stronger now than ever before?

I want to challenge you to stop prioritizing what others think about you. I know, this is hard. You've been programmed to think you aren't good enough, so of course you would think others feel that way too. If you're already saying "so what" then you are on the right track. But I hope to inspire you to redefine how you speak to yourself. Do the things that make you happy and do them for you. Think about why your decisions are true for you. A "so what" mindset places an emphasis on me vs. them. A "what-if" mindset only lives within you. Nurture the life that is true for you, and don't worry about anyone else.

There's a little bit more I'd like you to know about this story, and that has to do with the number on the scale. I almost didn't want to write about my relationship with my weight, because really in many ways it's an irrelevant part of my story. But I know I am not alone in having feelings of being less than just because I weigh more than. Before you read any more about this topic, I want to remind you: you are perfect as you are, and so am I. Your weight is not a part of your story. It's JUST A NUMBER and it has nothing to do with who you are and what you are capable of.

Along with all the other things that were happening in my life while transitioning away from my law enforcement career, I was also rapidly gaining weight. I want to be very clear that by speaking about my weight gain I am not being critical of myself. I had to work through a lot to accept myself at this size. After two babies and struggling with eating habits and anxiety, this wasn't easy. I'm in a good place now, but I went through a lot of worry over my body when it never needed to be a part of my dialogue.

I was embarrassed to come to my hometown. What if someone saw me? I didn't want to connect with old friends. What would they think of me? I know now that the people who care about me never really cared, and strangers likely never cared either. This doesn't mean that people don't care about me, but they don't care about what I weight. The people that are meant to be in your life will never make you feel less than for having a shift in size. What you really need to know about this part of my story, is that this part of my story doesn't matter. I am not less of a person because my body is larger. I may not always be this size. I could be larger. I am no longer concerned with the number on the scale or the size of my jeans. I am so much more concerned with living for my children and being the best version of myself I can be.

I am so fortunate that I have never felt like someone I love doesn't love me because of my weight. I want you to know that if you have someone in your life who is making you feel less than, you need to dissolve that relationship. You need to work on your relationship with yourself. You need to respect yourself enough to say no to relationships that aren't healthy. Be it a friend, a relative, or relationship or even an influencer on the internet. Your body does not define you and you are so much more than a number on a scale. Through everything that I had done in my life, the ups and downs, I had always had a background voice telling me that I had to be a certain way for people to approve of me. I had to dress a certain way, style my hair like everyone else, and make life choices for other people too. I don't think these thoughts came from a place of disliking myself. Instead, I truly feel that I sought the approval of others because I simply didn't know myself. I thought I knew exactly who I was supposed to be, and this meant I never allowed myself to explore who I could be. Maybe if I hadn't met key people along the way, like my amazing husband, I might be the person who I always imagined I would be. But I didn't sit still, I grew, and I changed into a person I am proud of. I truly believe that if you aren't growing you aren't living. You should be out there learning, experiencing, growing and changing. It might not always make sense to those around you, but you need to do this for you.

Don't ever make excuses for who you have become as you move through your life. You can change your mind and be someone you never thought you would be. I didn't know that I would love being a mother. I didn't know that I wanted to be present at every family event. I didn't know that I would like teaching young children. I didn't know that I would ever be an author of a book. I didn't know any of this, but I am so proud of myself for allowing myself to change and be the person I needed to be. Let go of shame from your past. Let go of shame from your present. You are worthy of being happy now and you do not need to explain yourself. I wish I could have told myself all these things at the beginning of my story. But I had to live these experiences instead. I know so much more about myself by letting myself fail and rebuilding my life. I am now so optimistic for a future that has so much more change to come. I know that failure is okay and that it can even lead into something better than you could ever imagine.

I don't think that my story is anything special. I am a regular person, with a very normal life. I haven't faced extreme adversity or tragic circumstances. If anything, I've had it easy. But my story is my story and it matters. Everything I have ever felt is valid and there is no need for comparison between my story and anyone else's. I want you to know that this applies to you, too. Whether you have overcome monumental feats or have simply been moving through life at a comfortable pace, your story is important. Your feelings are important. You are important. Don't allow anyone to make you feel like the journey of you is less than. I never thought I would be on this path today, but I am so happy that I am. I often think about what life would be like if I had gone another route and forced the path that didn't feel right. I no longer feel saddened or ashamed about not being the person I thought I would be. Instead, I am excited about what the future holds. I love the life I have created. I love the people I share it with and most importantly, I love myself. I hope you too can find love in living for who you are, whether you know who that is yet or not.

KEY TAKEAWAY

Katherine Burk

@bibsandbudgets
@momfidentaf
#selfloveclub

PART II:

Life Events and Experiences

Self-Love Realizations Through Childhood Trauma, Relationships, Parenting, Motherhood, Health and Fitness, and Self-Image

CHAPTER SEVEN

Milli Fox

Milli Fox is a writer, book-worm, speaker, influencer and entrepreneur from Toronto, Ontario. Milli and her family of three (soon to be four!) love to travel and you can often find them in Miami, specifically. She is super passionate about helping women rediscover their most vibrant selves and does so through her fun and inspiring online presence, mostly on Instagram and YouTube. In her early years, Milli studied psychology, pre and post-natal fitness as well as fertility nutrition. She is a huge advocate for healthy living, mind, body and soul, especially for women on their journey into motherhood. So much so, that she also became a doula. After having her son in 2017, Milli launched a ring sling business called Junior Foxes, catering to new moms who want to feel a sense of their own personal style while being empowered to get more done in a day. In 2019, she was named "one to watch" by the Mompreneur Awards. It's on this exact same wave-length that Milli does most things, empowering women to be themselves and take on the world. Self-love and compassion are always the undercurrent powering her to help more and more women.

Find Milli:
@millifox | www.millifox.com
@juniorfoxes | www.juniorfoxes.com
Author Photo: Josie Cipriano

Self-love is an interesting thing. Like many concepts, it's dynamic and there are so, so many things that go into it. In my experience, self-love doesn't happen in a vacuum. There is this popular idea that you have to go off on a solo eat, pray, love worthy mission to learn how to love yourself. But I think that's unrealistic and almost a form of martyrdom. But maybe it's just a side-effect of our highly individualistic society. Heck, it could even be a form of procrastination! What I know is that my journey didn't happen alone. I learned how to not love myself as a variety of coping mechanisms acquired during childhood in a family setting. And I learned to re-love myself surrounded by a crew of extremely loving individuals, cheering me on.

My story of self-love is a long one. I've shared it with a select few people, and shared sprinkles of it on social media and on my blog. But I truly believe it's part of my "raison d'être"[4] to share these experiences so that other women can see what's possible and also so they can know that they aren't alone. Even when we think our problems are incredibly unique and that no one else feels the way we do, there's always someone who gets it.

There was once a time when I was afraid to share my story. It's kind of funny looking back and realizing that's

4 "Reason for being"

truly how I felt because I've always self-identified as an outspoken person. I remember vividly walking through the park behind my house at about eleven years old in late fall. I was thinking about writing a book one day and how it would turn my life upside down if I shared all the stories that I'd already accumulated at such a young age. My mom would be furious. Her family would be outraged. Lives would be turned upside down. But even then I knew that it was going to be a part of my journey. I always somehow knew that I was meant to go through so many difficult and sad things so that I could share them to help other women.

My self-love story begins with my foundation; the place we are *supposed* to gain a sense of safety and stability, my mother. I come from generations of deeply wounded women. The irony of it is, on my grandmother's dying day, she said to my mother: "Make sure you don't treat Emily the way I treated you." Don't get me wrong, I truly believe my mother tried her best; it's part of my core belief that people are generally trying their best with the tools they have. The wonderful thing is, now-a-days we have SO MANY new tools at our fingertips and opportunities to run head-first into healing. That's what I've done.

A little back story: my mom was raised by abusive alcoholic parents, and she was sexually abused throughout her childhood. Her own mother refused to acknowledge what was happening. My mom tried her best to break free from the trauma and the pain, and she did what most people try to do as a first attempt to be different from their families: she tried to be perfect. She left home at 15, got married to my father at 19 and then impressively, she was able to earn a college degree in fine arts and then started her own graphic design business. She was super health-focused, spiritual, in great shape, and had two children by the time she was 28. From the outside, she looked like she had crafted herself the perfect life. On top of it all, she was gorgeous, charismatic, and had a ton of friends.

Unfortunately, all the pain she had swept under the rug slowly started to seep out and poison her and everything around her. My grandmother died two weeks before my younger brother was born when she was just 28, and the grief mixed with the hormones sent my mother into a severe postpartum depression. The first time she tried to take her own life, my brother hadn't even turned one yet. She never asked for help. She never shared her suffering, she just kept on trying to push it down, numb it, and deny it.

Then the cocaine happened. Her and my dad enjoyed partying together, but they just didn't realize how dangerous that was for my mother. It was a slippery slope for her to say the least.

For the majority of my early childhood, I remember my mom being on the couch. She would complain that she was in pain because she had ovarian cysts, but I think it was often her covering up the fact that she was nursing a deadly hangover and battling her newly acquired cocaine addiction. During this time, my father and mother decided to experiment with swinging, but that experiment evolved into a full-on affair between my mother and my best friend's father. One that she later blamed me for (even though I was in kindergarten at the time).

So, this was my beginning. Although I must acknowledge that I did get almost three amazing years with her before she hit her wall. She threw herself into the role of motherhood and she really did try her best. I've heard so many stories about what a dedicated mother she was and how much she poured into me. I will never forget to acknowledge this and I send that young woman so much love. Now that I've had time to reflect on it all, I see that she tried to find healing for herself in that role. But what I was missing was her ability to see herself as a dynamic and talented women worthy of love despite how well she was able to fulfill any one certain role.

What I also know now from my own experiences, is that it's a fatal effort to try to gain love, validation and acceptance through how well you can perform. Perfectionism is celebrated in our society. But what I've learned is that where perfectionism exists, shame is is the one pulling all the strings.

I'm not sure when I became her enemy, but boy did I ever. In fact, she would even tell me that in a past life, my brother was her ally and I was her enemy. It was those kind of thoughts that programmed me to believe that I could never be good enough, that I was never loved unconditionally. She would actually tell me that *I* didn't have the capacity to love, that I was difficult, a little brat, I would never be able to hold a job because I'd be fired for my attitude problems. She would tell me I was cold, just like her own mother, and that I never wanted to cuddle her even when I was a baby and that proved to her that I was incapable of warmth and love. She even told me that I had abandoned her since the day I was born- because I wasn't how she needed me to be.

She told me so many things about myself, that my little heart just kept piling it on as evidence that I wasn't inherently good enough and that I would need to prove to the world how incredible I was with my achievements. It's kind of crazy that when you want to be so different from someone that sometimes you get to a point where you look in the mirror and you're put flat on your ass by the realization of how closely you end up resembling them. This has happened to me more than once in my 30 years.

The first time this happened was when I was 19 and I had met my soon-to-be husband. I was finishing a degree in University, and paying my own way with basically a full-time job at the same time. I had a moment where I realized I was in the exact same spot my mom was at that time in her life, so I dove head first into the world of self-help. I was addicted; I was a self-proclaimed self-help junkie. I read all the Deepak Chopra and Eckhart Tolle and any other big name in that realm that I could get my hands on. I would get a high off each book and felt good about myself for the fact that I was evolved enough to seek out this type of guidance; I thought I was safe and I thought I was doing it better than she did.

I even went to University to pursue a degree in psychology. I was determined to get my PhD in psychology and become a clinical psychologist so I could figure out mental illness and put an end to it. To be different from her.

I did this out of a need to control. I felt chaos inside so I tried to make everything on the outside as neat and tidy a possible. This behaviour stemmed from the deeply rooted perfectionism that by this point had penetrated every area of my life. In high school, I had reached the peak of it. I maintained a 94% average and I took advanced courses. I was on student council, I was on the swim team, I was in three choirs, I ran my own club, and I even had a long term boyfriend and a part-time job three nights a week that I took public transit to and from no matter what the weather. I did it all without any help or recognition. I tried to check all the boxes. My parents didn't seem to care that much about what I was up to, so I just kept pushing for excellence so I could gain the recognition (which felt as close to love as I could get) from other places. All the while having my dad refer to me as "little-Paula" (my mom), which just stoked the fire to prove I was different even more.

It was my mission to get a scholarship and save up enough money to get out of my mother's house as soon humanly possible. The summer after I graduated high school, I moved out. At age seventeen. I was (and still am) *so* proud of myself for that.

I should also mention that while I was in high school my mom met her next husband, who turned out to be an abusive alcoholic. While she was married to him, she developed a new addiction to opioids and would mix them with alcohol. Those were the years where her abuse towards me escalated and became more violent.

When my mother's husband died of a heart attack in their en-suite washroom at the age of 52, I was in grade eleven. My mom was on chemotherapy for Hepatitis C at the time, and she never fully recovered from the loss of her abuser, or her own health. Neither did our relationship.

However, I somehow kept my chin up and my eyes on the prize through it all. I even wrote an award winning essay about finding my step-father dead on the floor. Talk about a way to cope!

Along the way I picked up a couple of numbing habits that I thought were harmless. Everyone else I knew was doing the same things, and I justified it as a normal part of being a teenager. I mostly smoked weed. I drank a bit as well, but the weed was something I could do and still function. So I did that. I smoked every day. I would even smoke before going to work and going to school. I would smoke before exams and when I got home at night. I smoked every day until I met my now husband.

When we met I was 19; I had just moved to Toronto and was working as a server full time. I took a year away from university to work and my plan was to move back to my hometown of Waterloo and complete my degree after the year had passed. However, I just loved Toronto way too much. I felt like I could be myself there, I loved the anonymity, and how it felt to break away from all the layers of embarrassment and trauma that I left back in Waterloo. I decided pretty quickly not to go back. Plus the farther I could get from my mom, the better.

Junior, my now husband, didn't smoke weed. He didn't like it. Since I was pretty much head over heels for him from day one, and obviously ripe for codependent tendencies, I didn't mind dropping it on a dime. Which I am still 100% happy about to this day. The thing is, though, that's when I started drinking more. Junior enjoyed imbibing, and he's seven years older than me, so he had money to buy alcohol at the bar or restaurants when we went out. It always seemed to be around, so it was a slippery slope for me. Especially considering alcoholism runs deep in my family.

For many years, I believed my drinking was normal. Despite the fact that I didn't know when to stop; that I was often the last one still drinking; and that I would continue to drink when we got home from the bar at 3am… I thought it was "just drinking" and not a big deal. I didn't listen when I was told it was too much or I should cut back, or that I couldn't handle my alcohol. I just wrote it off like all the other criticisms that I was so used to hearing from my mom.

Then, when we moved to the suburbs, and we didn't have the bars to go out to so I could get my fill of partying and drinking… I just started drinking at home. Alone. It got worse and worse. I needed to drink, and I would drink anything and everything. I would stay up several nights a week after Junior went to bed (even though he would always plead with me to come with him) and I would drink and smoke cigarettes until I'd need to run to the spare bathroom and throw-up, hoping I wasn't heard before crawling into bed and fighting the spins as I tried to fall asleep.

I hid how much I would drink. I would sneak into the kitchen quietly and take swigs out of whatever was there. I remember some particularly unappealing options being over-proof rum that someone gifted us as a joke and terrible homemade wine. At family events, I would volunteer to clean the kitchen so I could drink all the leftover sips of wine that people didn't finish from their glasses. It didn't matter to me what I was drinking or where it was from. As long as it numbed, it worked.

While all of this was happening, I was still reading all the self-help books. I had also become a personal trainer and was studying nutrition. I still *felt* like I had everything under control. And it looked that way to most people.

We decided to move back downtown around the time I was about 25, and something happened. I went too far. My drinking led me to make some really terrible decisions that almost ended my marriage. There was no infidelity involved, but there was dishonesty and betrayal.

That was my wake up call.

That's when I realized that I wasn't okay.

That's when I knew, that what I had been calling healing was actually just spiritual bypassing. If you're not familiar with the term, it basically means you are going through the motions of healing but you're not actually getting to the core of the trauma and shadow work that actually needs to be done. Think of it as the yoga-obsessed person that still does drugs and binge drinks on the weekend. They're kind of missing the point.

At this point I was desperate. I was deathly afraid to lose the first person who ever fully saw me for who I was and loved me for it. So I was extremely committed to getting help. For the first time ever, I started therapy. I quit binge drinking and I started really examining my own behaviour.

I started journaling, a lot. I started "doing the work" instead of just intellectualizing all my problems. I covered our condo with affirmations. I practiced new ways of speaking to myself and wrote messages on Post-its that I stuck to the bathroom mirror. I communicated my feelings daily to Junior and I learned how to start expressing my needs and how I wanted to be spoken to.

After months and months of deep work, and huge feelings of vulnerability and tenderness, things started to change for me. Junior and I felt like we had entered a new chapter of our relationship and I felt like I was truly starting to "grow up". I was very lucky to have an extremely supportive partner that was there to hold space for me while I dove into this difficult and painful work. I really cracked open all of the hateful beliefs I had been harbouring about myself that I didn't ever want to recognize were there. I didn't *know* I had a self-love deficiency until I was able to realize that I had been acting in an extremely self-sabotaging and loathing way.

The next year, we decided the timing was right and I became a mother myself. It was a huge shift for me. I had Rosen, my son who is now almost three, at home without medication. There was something about experiencing my own raw power to create and birth another human that made me realize how incredibly strong I am.

I've accomplished so much since becoming a mother. I've started and grown Junior Foxes, a ring sling country that's internationally recognized. I've started coaching other women through individual and group settings. I've gone straight towards what I wanted and proven to myself time and time again I am capable and I am worthy.

I won't lie, this journey has been hard *af*. It's been triggering *af* and I've had to recommit to my own healing several times since.

My second wave of deep healing came after another slip up. In August of the year before my son turned two, I attended my cousins wedding. Her mom had terminal cancer, and they were best friends. My cousin had moved up her wedding date to ensure her mom was able to attend before she passed. Watching them together in their beautiful relationship that was tragically nearing the end was extremely triggering for me. It unleashed a huge wave of grief and sadness for me. Sadness for them, and also for my own lack of a relationship with my own mother, which I feel every person deserves to have. I drank way too much that night and wasn't able to take care of my own son.

I slept on the bathroom floor next to the toilet and felt incredibly disgusting and ashamed the next day.

That was the last time I got drunk.

I started therapy again with a new therapist and really started to focus on me. I journaled, a lot. I leaned in to the work even more and I dedicated myself to both learning to love myself fully and letting go of any expectations I had for my relationship with my own mother.

I mourned the loss of our relationship.

I learned about boundaries. I learned about self-trust and self-abandonment and the crucial roles they play in self-love. I learned about co-dependency. I learned about myself. I focused on exploring what I like, what lights me up. What makes me feel like me and what pains or fears are lurking behind the anger.

A few things that have been integral to my healing have been lots of therapy, *The Gifts of Imperfection* by Brene Brown (I've read it at least 6 times in the last year and a half), the concept of Human Design, and always going 7 layers deep in my personal inquiry and journalling it out. Yoga, meditation, taking care of my body through good nutrition and movement as well as nurturing intimacy in my closest relationships.

Is my journey complete? Hell, no. It's just begun, and my healing is fresh. Has my life changed completely in the last five years? Hell, yes. I feel at home in myself. I feel as though my own abilities to comfort myself are the most important.

I let go of debilitating anxiety.

I'm now the self-proclaimed Queen of "Good-Enough".

I'm nowhere close to where I want to be; I still fight with comparison, I still fight with not good enough. But at the same time. I've been finding it so much easier to give myself a pat on the back and be my own biggest cheerleader. With a baby girl of my own on the way, I can feel another huge wave of healing approaching me quickly.

I try my best speak kindly to myself often and I choose to slow down and act with compassion and courage as often as possible.

I'm dedicated to living a wholehearted life as a resilient woman. I'm dedicated to self-love and I know that it's a lifelong commitment.

I know I'm here to break the cycle of familial trauma, and I feel so honoured that I've had the privilege and circumstances to be able to do so. I don't think you arrive at self-love, I think you discover it like a new land and you keep getting to know it on a deeper and deeper level the longer you choose to live there. It becomes a familiar place, and it becomes a place of deep comfort. It becomes home.

Like I said at the beginning of the chapter, self-love doesn't happen in isolation. I didn't do it alone. It took seeing the reflections of myself in others, their honest feedback about my behaviour (as painful as it may have been) and their decisions to stand by me all the while (but also sometimes not...) that brought me to where I am.

It also took my courage to be vulnerable. To keep choosing to be open rather than to shut down and put my walls back up. It took learning how to feel my emotions, dive seven layers deep into them and to learn how to start sharing my feelings without turning them into an attack on someone else or myself.

It takes dedication. It takes grit.

It takes wanting something different for yourself so badly that you are relentless in your ability to stand back up no matter how many times you fall. Kissing your own boo-boos and being the parent that you always needed.

And I believe you can do it. I believe anyone can.

Babe, welcome yourself to the self-love club, 'cause just by choosing this book, you're already a member.

If you want to come and learn more about my day-to-day journey, what I'm currently working on and indulge yourself in some more of my insight, I would be absolutely thrilled to have you come and follow me on Instagram **@millifox** or to have a peek at my site **www.millifox.com**

KEY TAKEAWAY

Milli Fox

@millifox | @juniorfoxes
@momfidentaf
#selfloveclub

CHAPTER EIGHT

Amy Jacobs

Amy Jacobs is a fitness and life coach for women who is passionate about holistic health and raising strong, confident girls. She lives in Miami, Florida with her husband and two young girls, with a third on the way (Due June 2020). Amy studied Dance and Education in college in NYC and built a decade long career in the city teaching dance, coaching gymnastics and leading teams of other passionate teachers and coaches before launching her own coaching business in 2018 after the birth of her second child. She is now a homeschooling, business-owning Mama who enjoys indulging in the beautiful Miami weather with her family and can most often be found working out with her mini girl-squad.

Find Amy:
@amyljacobs

"You mean, she'll always have two different coloured hands?"

There's so much about bringing a tiny human into the world that nobody really talks about. The things that our bodies and minds go through from the moment of conception to long after that human is actually here—it's complete insanity. Miraculous, sure. Awe-inspiring and powerful? Absolutely.

But it's completely freaking crazy.

For me, the chaos started right away. The day that I found out I was pregnant, I promised myself that I was going to stay 'fit'. Admittedly, I wanted to be one of those cute pregnant women who only looked pregnant when she turned to the side and you could see the basketball that she was smuggling under her perfect little maternity dress. I saw it every day. I was a District Manager at the time for an Early Childhood Education company in New York City. The mothers that I worked around all had that look. I watched them bring children into the world and into our locations for years and we admired how fit and fabulous they appeared to be. I wanted to be them. Having danced for most of my life and then turning that passion into a love for fitness, I figured: I've got this. Easy peasy.

A few days after the positive pregnancy test, I was hit with the completely debilitating all-day sickness. ('Morning' sickness? Yeah right. Who even coined that term?) It started the moment I woke up in the morning and followed me all over New York City where I was riding the rails between Jersey, Brooklyn, Manhattan, and Queens because I spent a huge portion of my day on the subway commuting between my locations. I got really good at knowing where to position myself on the train so that there would be a garbage can right in front of the doors when they opened that I could throw up in.

The only thing I could tolerate for months was carbs. I lived on New York City bagels and pasta. After long days of commuting, teaching, training, strategizing, coaching, and everything else that fell under the umbrella of my position, I commuted about two hours home on more trains and busses. The thought of working out felt like a death sentence. I binged on something sugary to satisfy my physical and emotional fatigue and lounged on the couch in between trips to bury my head in the toilet bowl.

The weight piled on FAST. Even into the second and third trimesters, I really took the whole 'I'm pregnant, I'll eat what I want!' concept to new heights. Fast food, take out, delivery - anything I once considered an indulgence became everyday life. I gave into every craving and whim in absolute excess. I honestly didn't even see it happening. In my mind I was still, well, ME. I was still the former dancer and fitness fanatic. It wasn't until I saw a picture of myself from a baby shower that I was hit with the reality of how much I had actually gained. I started dreading going to my regular prenatal check-ups because I knew that the scale was going to terrify me with numbers I'd never even thought possible for myself.

What I didn't know was all of the other complications that would start to arise. Borderline gestational diabetes. Gestational hypertension. Bed-rest. Being monitored weekly for signs of preeclampsia which would eventually show and force me into an induced labor and eventual c-section, squashing all of my dreams of a completely natural and unassisted birth.

So now, before even becoming a mother, nothing was going according to plan. The idealized "fit and cute" pregnancy I fantasized about was a complete joke. I had gained 60 pounds. The beautiful and natural delivery I saw for myself was a total disaster.

Through it all though, she arrived. Our first baby girl, Remy. But as quickly as I heard her cry, I heard the concern in the doctors' voices. Something was wrong. In my haze I could barely understand what was happening. I'd laboured unmedicated for two days with no progress before giving into the epidural a c-section. Something was wrong with her hand. It was dark. Maybe it was a dead hand, maybe the cord had gotten wrapped around it, maybe burst blood vessels, they didn't know. But they took her away for testing while I was still splayed open on the operating table.

What followed would be one of the longest nights of my life. I couldn't go see her or hold her. I needed to rest and recover and nothing could be done until the specialists came in the next morning. I woke up desperate to go see her. First, I needed to be examined. Waiting. Then, they had to take the catheter out. More waiting. I started fighting with the nurses to let me go but *apparently* it was super important for me to be able to pee on my own first. Sexy, I know. I've never been more determined to do anything in my life. Finally, I was in a wheelchair all ready to go when the team of doctors came into my room and sat on my bed across from myself and my husband.

Was the hand dead? Would she lose it? Is it just some burst blood vessels and this will all go away?

I sat in the wheelchair, more desperate to just go be with her than anything else, and listened to them tell me that Remy had a congenital melanocytic nevus - essentially a really large birthmark. She also had 'satellite' birthmarks all over her body - smaller versions on her elbow, scalp, butt cheek and groin. But the largest was her hand - a little black glove that would always grow with her.

I looked at these two doctors, women who showed very little empathy or compassion, and asked: "You mean, she'll always have two different coloured hands?" Yes. Yes, she would. And she'd need MRIs in the hospital to ensure none of the cells that caused the birthmark had traveled to her brain and would need to be monitored her whole life for melanoma. I suppose I should have felt relieved that it wasn't more serious, but I was heartbroken. All I could picture was her future in school or on the playground, getting made fun of for her hand. Her running home to me with tears in her eyes because she was different. I felt that pain deeper than I did any single contraction, the epidural or the recovery I was currently dealing with. I let my husband wheel me down to her in the NICU with a heavy heart.

But then I held her. Holding her was like holding a piece of myself that had gone missing. We fit together like puzzle pieces and even though I didn't feel that rush of love that so many other new moms talked about, I felt a fire inside of me. An urge to protect her. To guard her from whatever life would throw her way.

In that moment, my own needs moved to the back of my mind.

I've heard it said so many times, in ways far more eloquent than I could ever write myself: that with the birth of a child a mother is also born. A whole new version of a person that was a full-fledged human before she ever brought another one into the world. I remember someone sending me that article when I was pregnant with my first child and thinking to myself, *Yeah right. I've got this. I'm not going to change. This girl is coming into MY life - not the other way around.*

I should have known...

I should have seen from the moment I got pregnant that I was becoming a whole new version of myself already. And for me, unfortunately, I was dismantling the woman that I had always been brick by brick—and not in a positive way.

The girl who grew up dancing and loved the feeling of constant movement on her body. The college arts student who was convinced she could leap as high and travel as far as the men in her professional dance classes and that being a woman couldn't stop her. The gymnastics and dance coach who could handle a room full of 2 year olds in leotards without breaking a sweat. The fitness instructor who prided herself on pushing her clients to their absolute limits while pushing her own right alongside of them. The gym rat who saw someone lifting weights and convinced herself that she could lift heavier. The corporate woman who was always pushing for the next goal, the next position, the next rung on the ladder. That woman was becoming a shadow.

It started early on, when the morning sickness crashed over me. I was completely unprepared for what pregnancy would do to my body and I let that become my identity. Pregnancy defined me and I would often think to myself, *I'll get it all back once she gets here. I just have to get through this.* I was less prepared for the pain and difficulty of recovery. For how little time 12 weeks actually is and how ridiculous the idea of 'bouncing back' is in reality.

Then, there was this little girl that caught me completely off-guard. Motherhood started to define me in a whole different way. Let's face it, as new mothers, we are pretty much clueless. Advice is raining down on us from every possible source, and so much of it conflicting. We are attempting to recover from everything that our bodies have been put through and battling raging hormones while keeping a tiny human alive on absolutely zero sleep and even less of an understanding as to how. For MONTHS. It's insane. Add on top of that the emotional toll of handling all of the questions and comments that were flying at me about something that I'd barely wrapped my head around, myself:

"What's wrong with her hand?"

"Can anything be done about it?"

"Maybe it will just go away."

"My cousin had a birthmark like that but you can't really see it anymore."

"How are you going to handle that?"

"She's going to have a lot to deal with as she grows up..." (Yeah, no shit. Thanks!).

That urge to protect her grew in my gut like the ball of fire that gathers in a dragon's mouth before she explodes - and I was ready to shoot it at anyone. I felt like all anyone saw when they looked at her, this beautiful little human that I'd created, was her hand. I started keeping it covered with little hand mitts under the pretence that they were there to prevent her from scratching herself. I snapped at anyone who asked about it. "It's just a birthmark! And she's beautiful!" I'd snap, even if their intentions were completely pure. They didn't stand a chance against my fire.

A new identity was falling on me - one of a fierce protector - and I wore it with pride. I felt like a superhero, there to defend my daughter against a cruel and judgemental world. And when the time came for me to return to work, I felt confident that I could handle it all. I was super-mom, after all.

I slipped right into working mom mode and back into my busy corporate life. I took all of the bad habits that I'd accumulated during pregnancy and postpartum life with me. I was far too exhausted and overwhelmed to think of making a change. I juggled a high-pressure career, still trying to grow and hit goals, all while rushing home into new-mom life after long meetings and longer commutes. That fierce protective shield that I'd donned in those postpartum months came with me and I started using it to defend myself against perceived judgements, whether they were there or not. I was out to prove something and ready to fight against anyone who questioned my ability to "do it all."

In reality, I was drowning. The shield I was wearing was presenting itself to the world as anger, intimidation, dissatisfaction, confrontation, and a trying attitude. I was struggling at work with crazy levels of stress and anxiety. I brought a short temper home with me to my husband and my daughter. I was exhausted and overwhelmed at all hours of the day, even when it came to sleep (or lack thereof). I buried my pain and my emotions in food and kept seeking outside sources to ease the suffering of what felt like constant failure. Nothing was ever enough. I was never enough. I kept fighting for the next promotion, for a better apartment, for more money, and then found myself pushing for another child.

When I got pregnant again, I said to my husband, "It's got to be different this time. I've got to ease up on the stress and take care of myself. I've got to be healthier. I'm going to be." The challenge was that I had done zero work on myself to set myself up for success. I was so vigilant about protecting Remy from the world and protecting myself from what others might think that I didn't have the energy for anything else. There wasn't a single healthy habit to be seen anywhere in my life.

So pregnancy number two wasn't much different than the first, except that I got full-fledged preeclampsia this time around and Sydney came into the world as a preemie. She was, thankfully, extremely healthy and came home from the hospital with no issues. Until about a week or so, all seemed normal, then we noticed the bright red mark developing on her upper lip that grew with each passing day. By the time she was a month old, she had a large hemangioma on her upper lip that was partially obstructing her airway—another rare birthmark, this one more common in children born premature.

A few days after learning all there was to learn about *another* type of birthmark and getting Sydney started on a medication that would help her, I was at the playground with my husband and both girls. Remy was almost two, playing on the equipment with a couple of girls a few years older than her and I had Sydney wrapped against my chest in a carrier. I was chatting with another mom, explaining about Sydney's lip and how it was a mark that would go away in time while out of the corner of my eye,

I watched Remy play. I was so apprehensive. The older girls were asking Remy what was wrong with her hand, poking at it and then running away from her. She didn't yet have the language to speak up for herself so, instead, she walked over to me and sat next to me on the bench. She'd gone from happy and playful to completely shut down in an instant. She refused to go back and play, and my heart was completely broken. This was the moment I had been dreading. My husband and I just looked at each other and started walking the girls home.

That night, after we got them both bathed and in bed, I completely fell apart in his arms. I sobbed, knowing that this was going to be Remy's new normal and now her sister would face similar challenges in her early years as well. I didn't know what to do or how to help them. Neither one of us did. I felt in my bones that trying so fiercely to protect them against it was futile - that I had to do more for them. I had to raise them with unshakeable confidence, with belief in themselves that could stand up against anyone or anything. I wanted them to always see in themselves what their father and I saw in them, to love themselves completely and to value that love above whatever the world may throw at them.

But there was no way that I could do any of that. All of my years in education had taught me one of the most profound and simplest truths about children - they learn by watching. They will mirror what they see far more than they will listen to what they are told. So I knew that no matter how often I told my girls that they were beautiful, strong, smart, capable, confident, and perfect as is - they needed to see it reflected in me. They needed to learn self-love from their mother. Unfortunately, their mother didn't have much of it to show them. She was lost. She'd spent the past few years putting herself on the back burner and forgetting who it was that she truly wanted to be. She felt like she had nothing to offer.

The next day, I ripped off a piece of scrap paper from a notebook and wrote out a list of goals—something I hadn't done in years. I dusted off my old goal-setting techniques from the archives of my memories and got to work strategizing a plan of what felt, at the time, like 'getting myself back.' I purchased my first ever at-home fitness program, bought a new journal, pulled all of my athletic wear out of storage and posted my goals up on the door to my closet where I could see them all the time.

The experience in the beginning was humbling to say the least. I for sure thought that it wouldn't take too long for me to get back into the swing of things. I'd been active most of my life, after all. But in that first week, I threw up during three workouts, cried during even more of them, and sustained injuries to my knees that left me unable to walk. I leaked milk through sports bras, suffered through the worst engorgement pain while trying to do jumping jacks, and completely lost my cool with the girls out of sheer exhaustion. I was sore and defeated. I wanted so badly to give up right then and there. Everything felt absolutely impossible.

But then I remembered Remy's face that day at the

playground. I looked down at her little hand, and then back up to the goals that I had posted on my wall. I would never want for her to give up on herself. I knew that I had to show her that I wouldn't give up on me, either. So, I kept going. I committed to another week and this time, decided to stop ordering takeout and eating fast food. I worked with a physical therapist who helped me ease back into working out with more support for my body and less pain.

After a few weeks, I felt a shift happening in me. A confidence was building inside of me and I was starting to feel more like myself again. I don't think I lost all that much weight in the beginning but the emotional burdens that I was shedding made me feel lighter than I had in years. I took to social media for the first time to start sharing a bit of my story. I knew that I wasn't alone in feeling so lost and out of control in my own body. I wanted to share so that I could be held accountable for sticking to my own journey, and maybe inspire someone else along theirs.

Remy started working out with me. Not because I pushed her to, but because she wanted to do it with mommy. I made a concerted effort to always be positive in the way that I spoke to myself during a workout. I'd go completely over the top shouting things like, "This hurts, but I can do it!" or "This is hard but I believe in myself! I am strong!" It all started sinking into my brain until I believed it, and in her little voice, Remy would shout the same things while Sydney watched us from her swing. I changed the way I was eating and fuelling my body. I started looking at food in a whole new way—as a way to take care of myself instead of feeding my emotions. I spoke to the girls about it, too, while I prepared meals.

The confidence in me continued to grow. I honestly hadn't even lost a quarter of the weight I'd put on, yet, but I started wearing things out of my closet that I hadn't put on in years because I FELT better. I didn't feel the need to hide anymore. My mom and others closest to me started commenting on how much happier I seemed. My husband and I were reconnecting in our marriage, hardly realizing that anything had been missing before.

I delved deep into the world of personal development. I felt my body strengthening and I was becoming so much healthier, I wanted to do the same for my mind. I started reading, using whatever down time I had to learn about tackling my mindset and my emotions. I poured over other women's stories, I implemented new habits and routines into our lives, and spent my evenings with my husband talking about our vision for the future of our family in a whole new light. Things started to seem...possible.

It wasn't long into this journey that we decided it was time for me to quit my job and stay home with the girls. I felt very strongly that they needed me with them, and that the path I was on was exactly where I was meant to be. I knew that going back to work would be toxic for me, for all of us really, so we decided that I would quit. It would be a struggle financially and I'd have to do something to earn income but with that decision, another weight lifted off of me. I realized that I had been allowing success at my job to define me, just as I had the other phases of my life - the pregnancy, motherhood, former dancer, fitness freak. As I stepped away from each of these identities, I realized that I was stepping more into myself.

I wanted to give my girls that realization from the beginning. I started talking to Remy more about her birthmark and giving her the language to talk about it herself. I became very conscious of how I spoke about my own body when I looked at it in the mirror, knowing that she was listening and watching my every move. As the weight continued to come off, the excess skin and stretch marks appeared in all their glory but I never let myself get down about them. I didn't want her to see or hear that from me. So, I became determined to love those aspects of my new body as well. I showed them to Remy with pride and told her that these were special parts of me that I got by bringing her and her sister into the world.

It took me a little over a year and a half to lose the 70 pounds I had gained over my pregnancies, and then some, and to shed all of the crap that came with it. I lost so much more than weight. I lost the need to fulfill anyone else's expectations for me or my life except my own. I ditched the crippling self-doubt and insecurity that was keeping me stuck in an unhappy version of myself. I shed the borrowed identities of who I thought I was supposed to be and learned to embrace who I am. The journey was sparked by my amazing daughter, her beautiful birthmark and the desire to give her confidence which arose in me a need to find my own.

There is no finish line here. I haven't won some race or stopped learning or growing. If anything, the pull to keep going only gets stronger and stronger. Especially now. As I write this, I am pregnant with our third child, another little girl. With each chapter of life that is opening before me, I see how I need to shift and adapt to take the best parts of me and apply them where needed. The past year was coloured by the launch of my own business where I coach women through their own journeys. This new chapter is asking me to step more fully into motherhood and further away from business or career. But I have discovered that none of those titles or things are what define me. I am who I choose to be, and how I choose to show up in the world. In my home, in motherhood, as a wife, a sister, a daughter, a coach, a friend. It's freeing to take life on that way - to be less defined by who you are "supposed to" be and more so by showing up as the truest and most authentic version of yourself.

Healthier, more positive habits are a part of my everyday day now. I love myself too much to let them go, and I'm insanely passionate about sharing them with my girls. I still workout with Remy, and Sydney has joined us now, too. We talk about nutrition and how to take care of our bodies. We strategize how to handle our emotions, we forgive each other's mistakes and learn to support each other better. We journal together and have a routine of saying nightly affirmations before bed:

I am strong.

I am confident.

I am brave.

I am kind.

I can do anything.

I love myself.

I can do it all with them, because I do it first for me.

When I sat down to write this, I asked myself over and over again: What is self-love to me? I wrestled with the concept because I see it looking so differently on different women. I didn't want to get it 'wrong'. But that's not what it's about at all, is it? It's about each of us. Our own individual stories and our own journeys. It's embracing your humanity. It's knowing that version of yourself—the highest, most powerful, most confident and very best version of you—and never allowing yourself to stop becoming that person. It's trusting that she's in there, in all seasons of life, and knowing that she won't always look the same so whole-heartedly accepting her as she is every step of the way. Because it's not about the way that you look, it's about how you show up, which will always reflect the way that you feel about yourself. And no one gets to decide that for you.

I love imagining the future of our world. I know that can seem very scary sometimes, but my version of the future is shaped by our children. They are strong, kind, confident humans who are impacting and changing the world for the better. They've never known any other way, because they learned it from us—their mothers. Imagine that.

Two different coloured hands and all.

KEY TAKEAWAY
Amy Jacobs

@amyljacobs
@momfidentaf
#selfloveclub

CHAPTER NINE

Brittany Mowen

Brittany is a part-time stay at home mom, blogger and lover of DIY-ing. She lives in the small town of Greencastle, Pennsylvania where she recently began staying at home with her two kids after a seven year career as a Teaching Assistant in an Autism Support Classroom. God was moving her in a different direction, and she hasn't regretted it.

She started her blogging journey about two years ago. Throughout her journey learning the ins and outs of social media, she has discovered a passion for helping women be true to themselves by highlighting the feelings we all have about motherhood and self-image. She has been inspired by a lot of amazing people and enjoys spreading that inspiration back to her community.

If she isn't on Instagram, Brittany can be found working in her garden, doing fun projects with her kids, or creating new things in her craft room for her Etsy shop.

Find Brittany:
@mowen_manor | www.mowenmanor.com
Author Photo: Stephanie Maria Photography

I wish I could go back 15 years and tell myself that bodies are beautiful at any size.

That my weight will fluctuate many times over the next 15 years.

That there will be stretch marks and things that sag.

That I will go from bloated to feeling great and back again.

That the number on the scale or the size of those jeans doesn't matter. At all.

That even though I don't perceive myself as being beautiful, God does.

My self-love journey only began about a year ago. I had just turned 30 and still felt like I had no direction for my life. God had always been there to guide me but I hadn't been listening. There was a specific moment I remember. I was reading a Ted Dekker series called *The Outlaw Chronicles* (which I highly recommend) and the main characters in each book just spoke to me. The overall theme was about forgiveness and love and grace and redemption. I specifically remember a quote that hit me hard, in the book, *Eyes Wide Open*, after the main character had changed her physical appearance drastically, she finally opened her eyes to the truth. "It was her false self that was confused, thinking that it knew what ugly was and stewing in it, trying to be good enough when there was no such thing. The ugliness had been corrected a long time ago through forgiveness. It was time to forgive herself and surrender to the truth. She was complete, wholly restored without even a hint of any need for further correction."

I mean, wow.

God, thinks I am beautiful. The real me is safe in His arms and knowing that gives me the courage to be a little kinder to myself.

You are not your body. This is only a shell. A vessel. A costume.

The real you is the way you love and live and make the world just a little brighter. It's your soul. That part of you that no one can judge for being different. It's the part of you that is truly unique and makes you who you are.

After I read these books, I was in an entirely different place. The last 15 years or so had been a constant cycle of hating myself, dieting, still hating myself and then starting back over again. About a week after finishing that series I came across someone who made a huge impact on me. Her name is Sarah Nicole Landry, and her Instagram account (@ thebirdspapaya) just hit me square in the face. It was like a breath of fresh air and a face slap all at once. God knew exactly what he was doing and I couldn't be more grateful. My life has been forever changed because of a few books and one woman.

This self-love journey I started on began at the brink of spring and warm weather. Which obviously meant shorts, tank tops and swimsuits (yikes, am I right?). I dread this season. All that skin just hanging out for everyone to see. No, thank you. But, I was trying a different approach that year. I was going to put on what made me feel comfortable and cute and not let myself think about my cellulite or jiggly arms. Or those endless stretch marks from huge humans I squeezed out. I was going to let myself be free. You want to know what happened when I stopped worrying about what everyone else thought? My negative thoughts began to subside! I put on that swimsuit and played on the beach with my kids. I lived my life and made those amazing memories that easily could have been riddled with little nasty comments from my brain.

Be kind to yourself. I have learned to take this quote in deeper the last year of my life. We are taught and told to treat others as you would want to be treated. We like to be treated with respect and seen as someone worthy of another's time. But, do we turn that around? Sometimes I think it's harder to treat myself as well as I treat others. When you stand in front of that dressing room mirror do you smile and tell yourself that you look beautiful? Do you wonder at how amazing you look in that pretty floral dress? Or do you take one look and give a shrug of disgust at what is standing before you and try to imagine what it would look like if you just lost those 30 pounds?

I'm pretty sure every woman out there, no matter how 'ideal' of a body she has, has fought back those tears that well to the surface when you believe that you don't look beautiful enough.

As long as I can remember, I have struggled with wanting to change something about my body. I've daydreamed about it. Researched about it. Wrote down goals to get to my 'ideal body'. I've had what some would call that 'ideal body', but was I happy then? No. I still compared myself to those around me, still thinking I was fat. I've learned that your inner dialogue and thoughts about yourself are never going to change unless YOU do something about them. Don't start with the physical. Begin by stopping the talk about dieting or weight or anything negative about your body. Make observations about your body but don't pass judgement based on those observations. Eventually, your thoughts about all of that will begin to fade. I wish I could say that they go away completely, but I can't. I can tell you, though, that if you start small, with actionable steps, those negative thoughts and outward comments about yourself will change to just the negative thoughts. Then those negative thoughts will change to neutral thoughts. It's okay to feel neutral about how you look. Just eventually liking yourself a little bit is a step in the right direction. Self-love is the ultimate goal and it takes practice and effort to get there. Small steps toward that goal can mean the difference between living your life the way it was meant to be or forever waiting for something to improve. YOU have the power to change that. YOU are the one that decides if you sit on the side and watch someone else live the life you want. YOU alone can make the conscious decision to grab life by the handlebars and enjoy the ride. It's your life. Get out there and live it.

There's another point in my life that I remember being a sore spot for my body-image and self-love. The first was when it all started in middle school, but the second happened after I was diagnosed with Polycystic Ovary Syndrome and Hypothyroidism. This happened before I had my first baby I struggled a lot. I was in a very low place. The hardest was trying to get pregnant the first time. It had almost been two years and we were only months away from going to a fertility clinic. I hated myself and my body for betraying me. It was the hardest phase of my life.

I had gained weight, my skin was a mess and I had hair growing in places that it definitely shouldn't be. My hormones were a mess.

Fast forward to six years later and I still struggle some with the symptoms of PCOS. I don't have acne or hair growth as much anymore, but I still struggle with weight gain and hormonal imbalance. It's so, so hard not being able to control that as much as I feel I should. I feel like it's my fault and that I need to change. I'm always questioning myself. Why is my body turning against me? Why can't I control any of it? Why do I feel like I'm the only one? I'm sure a lot of you know how that feels. When our bodies go through things or we struggle with something mentally or emotionally, it can feel very isolating. It seems like we're the only person in the world going through it. People tell you to reach out and find others who have gone through the same thing who can support you, but truthfully that is hard. Who wants to bring their struggles to light and ask another person to help them? It can be humiliating. I never talked to anyone about it and I wish I would have. But, I never realized the support and community that can often be found online. If you are struggling with something that you don't know how to ask for help for, research different groups online. There are so many accounts on IG dedicated to supporting women and that focus on one type of struggle. There's help out there. You are not alone.

To be honest, everything you have just read, I feel inadequate to share. I truly do not feel equipped enough to tell another woman how she should love herself because my journey is still fresh. I'm still learning so much. But I think maybe that's the beauty in it. Each of us has our own story. Our own little part to tell. And to be able to have even the possibility of helping ONE woman realize just how worthy of it all she is, then these words are so worth it. Here's the thing, there's always that first moment in every female's life when they realize that they don't measure up to a certain standard they are seeing portrayed in the world. They begin to see that the body they have needs to be changed in some way or another to fit a mold that is before them. It's a tough pill to swallow knowing that society won't accept you JUST AS YOU ARE. This is the reason I am doing what I am doing. I want to change the world. Change it for those girls who see these lies; that the standards of beauty today are so unattainable that they will never measure up and that their worth is determined by their size.

I don't want this to ever happen to another girl again. It's so incredibly painful to think all those things that absolutely aren't true about yourself. And it's happening at a younger and younger age. I want these girls to NEVER have to doubt their worth as a human being or a woman. I don't want them to feel less than another woman when they look through a magazine or walk down the street and see a billboard or a swimsuit ad. There needs to be so much more change to get to that point. But it's happening slowly.

I can see it.

Acceptance of all the forms a woman's body can take is becoming more common and it's amazing to watch. I want my daughter to wake up every morning without the worry of whether or not you can see her cellulite or if when she sits down in those jeans if her tummy will have rolls or if she will be judged because she isn't a size two. Our future daughters and granddaughters hopefully will grow up in a world where they no longer have to fight for their acceptance. Where they no longer have to feel ashamed of what they look like. Where they can be free.

This is where diet culture is plaguing our hope of self-love. I want my daughter to NEVER feel like she needs to be different than she is. I don't want her to grow up in a house where dieting and constantly working out are praised. I'm tired of the comment, "You've lost weight! You look great!" This is why our society has so many eating disorders. It's the small comments whether positive or negative that draw attention to a person's size. It's those moments when a woman shares that she's going on a crash diet as soon as the holidays are over. It's the person looking at a photo and commenting on how fat they look and how they need to suck it in. It's someone saying, "Wow they've gained a lot of weight." WHY? How are these things okay? These comments are NOT compliments. They are damaging. They begin to mold that person's mind into thinking that looking a certain way will bring them praise and acceptance. We put so much of our identity into our physical appearance that it becomes all we see. We don't see how kind or loyal or thoughtful or sacrificial or giving or strong a person is. Because we are too focused on the outward appearance.

YOU ARE NOT A BODY.

Did you hear me?

YOU ARE NOT YOUR BODY.

Your body could be 20 different sizes and shapes in your lifetime and the person you are will remain the same. Sure, you will grow and change as you make memories and have experiences but, Who. You. Are. Is. The. Same. The truth is that our bodies will change and grow and shrink and move in so many ways that getting attached to a certain stage will harm how we look at our bodies in the future. I truly was never attached to my body during any stage. It was after the fact. When I was in high school, I thought I was fat. I tried to stay as thin as possible but my build was too 'sporty' and curvy in areas that it didn't allow me to do that.

After I had kids, I became attached to the pre-kid bod. I no longer thought it fat. Whichever state I was in at that moment was so horrifying that I thought I needed to change back to what I was before. The crazy thing is that I have grown so much and had so many memories made during those subtle changes with my body that I'm glad I couldn't go back. Right now, in this moment, I am glad my body changed how it did because I might not be as grateful for it or as amazed at what the human body can do.

All I'm saying is not to get too attached to what your body looks like. It's going to change so many times over the course of your life. Focus inward. Focus on what really matters. Focus on your heart and your spirit. Focus on kindness toward yourself and others. Focus on being the best human being possible. Once you shift that focus from outward to inward you will truly begin to realize what is important. You are a work of art. Your maker did not make a mistake when he formed you. I'm asking you to take little steps to start shifting your focus.

Stop commenting on a person's weight loss or weight gain.

Stop proclaiming that you are going to punish your body for the food you ate.

Stop saying how fat you look in photos or how much your belly sticks out.

Stop focusing on that double chin.

And start being kind to yourself and others.

Start changing the mantra and you'll start changing the world.

Speaking of focus, you know that feeling of nostalgia when all those memories suddenly come flooding back and you're back in that moment, that specific time in your life where everything just seemed right? I get these feelings a lot, especially around the holidays. Going on a hayride with my family, visiting haunted houses with friends in college, carving jack-o'-lanterns with my boyfriend, painting pumpkins with my kids. Then Christmas comes and it's the same feelings over all over again. It's those feelings of wishing for the good 'ole days. But we have to realize that we are actually *in* the good 'ole days. *Right now.*

You are in those moments now. The good 'ole days are happening right now. And one day you will look back and realize that you never truly lived because you were holding back. RIGHT NOW is your life. Not 6 months from now when you finally get in shape. Not next year when you feel like your finances are in order. Not in a few weeks after you have your house organized from spring cleaning. Life is happening NOW. Live it. Stop wasting precious moments and memories with the could-haves, should-haves, or may-have-beens. Don't wait for something to happen to start enjoying the life you were given.

And do not punish yourself for the memories you made and life you lived in the previous day, month or year. You made precious memories around tables full of friends and family while enjoying good food. You went on vacation and enjoyed all the meals because you didn't have to cook it yourself. It's okay to be okay with that. Don't spoil those memories by going on a crash diet. Let those times you laughed with family while eating that dessert fill your heart will warm thoughts. Let those moments with friends when you ate till your stomach felt like it would explode give you joy. Let yourself be okay with it. Why do we punish ourselves for the good things that happen in our lives?

Take a deep breath and bring those amazing feelings of closeness back without guilt of what filled your plate. You are more than a body. Your worth is more than what you eat. I've learned that you are not bad for eating unhealthy foods. Neither are you good for eating healthy foods. Take a neutral stance when it comes to what you eat. Eat what fuels your body and relish those moments when you indulge. It's not good or bad. Eat great food. Make great memories. Live a great life.

After all this though, I think I will always feel pressure to look better, like I was six years ago (pre-kids). I truly don't think that is ever going to change. And that's ok. I may not ever love my body completely. That's okay too. Body shaming is how I was raised. It's how my mom and dad were raised and it's probably how my grandparents were raised. It's the diet culture that has plagued our society for as long as I can remember. Moving on to the next best thing and changing ourselves to fit that mold. But here's the thing. That's not me anymore. That body from years ago isn't me. Our bodies ebb and flow with our lives and experiences and memories. And that's okay.

I just want to be in a place where I can celebrate what my body has done for me and appreciate what it continues to do. It moves and grows with each stage of life. It expands to form life and sustain life. It stretches to accommodate a growing human and that is beautiful.

Growing a person inside you is no easy feat. Your body does amazing things during those nine months and beyond. Don't let the world steal that from you. You are a warrior.

Here's where our postpartum bodies come into play. I'm two years postpartum as I write this. (That still counts as postpartum right? I mean, it's time after having a baby so why not?) Those initial three months, the dreaded 4th trimester, how do I say this...IT SUCKED! For me, it did, anyway. There's recovering from pushing a Saint Bernard out of your butt while trying to poop like a normal human being and also constantly having a baby attached to your boobs while leaking all over the place when he/she isn't. You have aches and pains and guilt and happiness and stress and feeling like a zombie from lack of sleep. That list is a thousand miles long. Who would have thought that three short months could hold so much.

But then you finally get out of that 4th trimester, and you start to feel a small sense of normalcy again. You might be going back to work or if you are staying home you begin to find a daily routine. But things just aren't the same. Your body is still not what it used to be. You're still sleep deprived. You wish you had the time or the energy to work out or even cook decent healthy meals on a daily basis. The house feels like it's NEVER going to be clean. You still have to pee constantly. And forget about holding it in when you sneeze. Body parts aren't where they should be anymore and you feel like you are living in someone else's body.

But let me tell you something. Those little human beings that you birthed don't care about any of it. To them you are their world. You can do no wrong in their eyes. Soak it all in, Momma. I read an article about coming back to work after maternity leave and the one thing that stuck with me the most was when the author said, "Whatever you do, just remember, you are doing the very best that you can for that little one. She is loved, she is cared for, and she is your number one. No matter what you do in life, if you keep these three things in mind, I promise you, it will be enough."

You, Mama, are enough.

Self-love isn't just about loving the physical part of yourself. It's also giving yourself permission to be okay with the imperfect human being you are. Those 'Pinterest moms' still don't have it all together. There's really a lot of pressure out there. Do you feel it? I do. It's like this overwhelming weight we feel to be more. It's normal and okay to want to improve yourself and your situation but what sucks is that the bar is ridiculously high. We expect too much of ourselves and each other. I wish I could shout from the rooftops that I have it all together. But, I'm not even close. (#hotmessexpress)

The reality is that my house is a mess more often than I'd like. I would love to have my floor spotless and everything in its place. But that's not my reality right now. My reality right now is two kids to take care of, a home to keep up and running, and a part-time job. My hubby is amazing at helping out, but it still takes a lot of time to do everything. I want to have my house spotless and everything put where it needs to be, but I don't have time for that right now. My standards haven't lowered at all, because I still dream of those spotless floors. But, my expectations of myself in this current stage of life have shifted. Because I know that with the spotless floors one day will bring no more squealing giggles and pitter pattering feet. I know that with things always in their place will bring no more kids laughter and joy as they play with their toys and make memories in our home. I know that with always having the laundry done will bring empty guest rooms...not kid's rooms and closets full of my children's treasures.

I'm not ready for that yet.

So for right now, I'll live with the crumbs on my carpet, the toys that are on the floor and mountains of clothes and I will love on my kids. I'm choosing to give myself grace. I'm choosing to forgive myself when I can't seem to keep it all together. I have goals for a great year but also grace for an unexceptional year. Because at the end of the day I know that all I really need to do is love God, love my family and love myself.

I want to leave you with these last thoughts. We don't

talk about the normality of the human body or psyche enough. We sit here behind our screens hiding the parts we don't want others to see. There's Photoshop and filters and cropping and just not letting anyone see the hard stuff. The stuff that hurts. The stuff that when brought to light seems forbidden. But the stretch marks, the anxiety, the tummy rolls, the depression, the hard "momming" days, hairy chins, PCOS, the self-hatred and acne are all normal. There isn't a woman out there who hasn't experienced something in her life she wants to hide from the world. This is why it's so important for us to share our stories. It's for those women who are coming up after us. So they don't have to climb mountains and fight battles just to be accepted as who they are. So that the world starts to learn forgiveness and the meaning of grace. They are powerful tools and can heal the most broken person.

As unqualified as I feel to be an author, I will NEVER stop sharing my story.

I am ready to change the world. Will you join me?

KEY TAKEAWAY

Brittany Mowen

@mowen_manor
@momfidentaf
#selfloveclub

CHAPTER TEN

Nikki King

Nikki King is a mom of four beautiful children, a Certified Personal Trainer and a Pre/Postnatal Fitness Specialist. Nikki is passionate about helping women recover their core strength after childbirth. She brings years of experience to her classes and truly understands the needs of her busy mama clients. Nikki recognizes the importance of a healthy active lifestyle, and thirsts to share her love for fitness and natural health with everyone she encounters.

Nikki is a former dancer, and loves sneaking alone time to go to aerial yoga or discover a new hiking trail. In between instructing classes and clients, Nikki is working towards completing her Holistic Nutrition Coach designation and keeping up with managing four littles!

Find Nikki:
@nikkikingfit
Author Photo: Stephanie Webster Photography

Sweaty palms. Shaking. There I stood up in front of 27 peers, giving a presentation on sexualization in the media, and its impact on youth and body image. I was only 17. Do you think I had actually internalized the dialogue I was presenting to my fellow peers? In short, no. I hadn't.

I spent weeks upon weeks researching for this project. I wanted it to be perfect. Almost as perfect as these women I would see in all the magazines I would often have stashed away in the corner of my bedroom, magazines featuring teen girls and women with the most perfect hair and makeup. Let's not even get started on their flawless bodies! If I did 200 crunches a day, I, too, could have the amazing abs that these women rocked! Right?

Screw the crunches, though! My form of exercise was walking to Harvey's with friends and shovelling a fork full of poutine to my mouth. I had often wondered why my co-workers at the grocery store I had worked at would comment on my lunch breaks about the meals I was purchasing. "You know, Nicole, you wait until you're our age and you can't eat whatever the hell you want. What will you do then?" At the time I would laugh and shrug it off, but I'll admit the words stuck with me. As the years went on those very words began to affect me in ways that I never thought they would.

It's crazy how we can turn a blind eye to all of these expectations that the media and society implants in our brains from such a ripe age. There are so many apparent "shoulds" in terms of the way we *should* conduct our day to day lives. How we *should* dress. How we *should* do our makeup. How we *should* do this fad diet or that one. How we *should* look, and how we *should* strive for skinny and perfect. It's this "should culture" that makes us crazy. It's not our bodies that are flawed. It's the unrealistic expectations that we impose on ourselves. With all these expectations, it's no wonder that people easily fall out of love with the skin they live in.

I, too, was that girl. The one who was eventually triggered by it all.

My 28th year was probably one of my hardest. I was a new mom to a busy toddler and a colicky newborn. My newborn son always cried. So much so, that at one point I had a complete stranger tell me at a grocery store that perhaps I should try feeding my child. Gee – thanks! I hadn't thought of that. To make matters worse, I survived on two to three hours of broken sleep a night for the first 9 months of his life. I couldn't catch a break.

My anxiety began to spiral out of control. I was a complete wreck.

A month shy of my son's first birthday, I was coming down from another anxiety attack. Grasping the bathroom counter, I reminded myself to stop rocking, stop shaking, and just breathe. I looked up in the mirror at myself to see this sad, helpless girl that I didn't recognize. I had lost touch with myself, and was often questioning my worthiness.

How could others love a girl who couldn't even find love for herself? I wondered often.

Many considered me to be a confident, fun-loving girl. They had no idea I was in the battle of my life with my inner demons. As days and weeks went on it became apparent to me that something had to give. I needed to do something for myself. I was miserable all the time. I hated the way I looked and how tired I felt all the time. I was at the heaviest weight I had ever have been.

Everyone I knew was putting themselves through the torture of Jillian Michael's "Shred" videos. I convinced myself to do the same. If the extreme results on The Biggest Loser were any indication, I was going to look fit and fabulous in no time! Pair that with making changes to my diet and I had myself the perfect prescription. At least I thought so. That first month, I focused on doing one of Jillian's workouts every day of the week. I "nourished" my body with a bowl of oatmeal for morning, a Slim Fast shake for lunch and whatever the hell I wanted for dinner. Generally, that was pasta slathered in way too much cheese. The more cheese the better, right? Each day often ended with me having a pounding headache that was unlike any other. I wasn't concerned though. This was just the initial detox phase, right?!

If I caved and had additional snacks or binged on something that I considered to be "bad" I would punish myself with more exercise. This is not a healthy cycle for anyone, but I fear a large percentage of women have been through something like this at some point in their lives, too. Sometimes we just don't know how to change our mindset to do better.

My exercise habits became more and more extreme as the months went on. It became my way of relieving stress. I had found out months earlier that my nana had been diagnosed with ALS. After her diagnosis, her health took a downward spiral fast. I was a mess. Knowing I was going to lose her affected me in ways that I don't think many realized. She wasn't just my nana. She was my best friend. Exercise became my coping mechanism. My workout routine looked a lot like a Jillian Michaels video (or two), an hour of Zumba and an hour on the stationary bike. Working out for an average of nearly three hours a day. I craved that endorphin high. It masked the immense pain I was feeling. No one had any idea how much I was hurting.

People started to begin commenting on how amazing I looked. Others voiced their concern, telling me to be careful not to wither away.

It was a complete mind-fuck.

Of course, I wrote those people off as the naysayers. They didn't know what they were talking about. I had everything under control. My diet. My exercise programs. Everything. What did they know, anyway?! They were just jealous. It was December of that year that things took a turn for the worse. I got that dreaded phone call. Nana only had a matter of days, maybe hours. Nothing ever prepares you for having to say goodbye one last time to a loved one. Only I never got to. She passed away the day before I was to see her one last time.

The whole world was crashing and burning around me. My life that had already been on a downward spiral completely crashed. My world went black. You never realize how hard grief can hit you until it punches you in the chest a couple hundred times in a row. It makes you feel so out of control of your own emotions and body. Food can often be an emotional and readily controllable source that can be taken advantage of when things seem overwhelming. Many women do this, unfortunately. Some people turn to emotional eating when they are feeling down and out; others decide to completely starve themselves. Both over- and under-eating are unhealthy for your body and your mind, and during this experience I was the under-eating person. The minimal appetite I had left became non-existent.

Weeks went on and I saw a significant change on the scale. The pounds came off, and I actually *celebrated* the unhealthy way I was living. I celebrated the fact that I wasn't eating, and that I was losing that last little bit of stubborn weight. What I didn't see was how sick I was making myself. I spent that Christmas in and out of doctors' offices with sickness after sickness. It was more important to me to celebrate the fact that in that past year I lost 60 pounds and was at the weight I once was in high school. It seemed like an incredible feat. Screw those co-workers who once told me it wouldn't be possible to maintain my teenage physique in adulthood.

It's funny how people seem to get it in their head that if they lose the weight and are skinny that they will be happier. I can tell you firsthand, it's *so* not true. I don't think there was ever a time I felt more down on myself than when I mistreated the one and only body I will ever have. Too easily, we can fall into this cycle of tricking ourselves with an illusion of that "should culture": how we *should* look, what we *should* eat, how we *should* act. We abuse our own inner-being with these horrible notions and when you fall down that rabbit hole, you become lost in it.

My wake-up call came about a month after Nana passed. It hit hard. What the fuck was I doing to myself? Where had I gotten this dangerous perception of what fit and healthy should look like? How could I possibly have tricked myself into believing that loving myself meant I would need to turn to such extremes? The vicious cycle of over exercising and allowing myself to malnourish my body had become so extreme that it wasn't sustainable. All these fads and diets never are.

It took a little while for me to start to feel okay with this realization. It's never easy to swallow the giant pill that you really screwed up. That you should have listened to those concerned naysayers because their concerns were valid. You just were so out of touch and blinded by your habits.

I started to work on shifting my mindset by creating new habits and manifesting the hell out of them. These habits I created were simple:

- Writing in a diary.
- Talking about my feelings.
- Taping a list of affirmations to the scale that I once obsessively stepped on multiple times a day.
- Standing in front of the mirror and saying one nice thing about myself.
- Allowing myself to eat and not feel guilty when I grabbed that scrumptious bag of chips.

It's now been seven years. A lot has changed. My body has a lot of new curves, rolls and stretch marks. All the things that once made me cringe that I'm now so proud of and learning to embrace. That girl in the mirror? I love her. She is strong. She is beautiful. She is capable. And those "tiger stripes", the ones that are forever a part of her, make her such a badass! My body housed four beautiful babies!

Sure - I still have days where I look at photos and pick myself apart. Those days when my stress spirals so out of control that I feel I'm losing touch with myself again. The days when I am reminded of those results I once saw by cutting dangerously back on calories and over exercising. It's times like those that it is so tempting to jump back on the bandwagon. Only I refuse, and I won't walk back into the worst season of my life.

I think the hardest thing for me has been looking back on those photos that pop back up in my Facebook memories from years ago. The same photos where many commented and told me how great I looked. All I can see is a sad girl beneath the disingenuous smile. A girl who was struggling to sort and put back together the pieces of her life. Only she couldn't figure it out. It brings me to tears every time I think of how much she was hurting inside, how she was struggling to weather the storm that no one knew about.

My wish is that no one ever feels the need to punish themselves for whatever emotional trauma they might be dealing with. It's times like that that it's okay to reach out for help. Whether it's therapy, going for a massage, a hot bath, or cozying up and reading a good book. Whatever a self-care routine looks like for you, do it. Just please don't ever fall down the rabbit hole I did.

It's okay to take a step back and breathe. It's okay to look in the mirror and want to love up on yourself, embracing your body for whatever journey it has taken you on. There may be bumps along the way, but that's all they are… minor hiccups. We can't let that define us.

Take care of your body – move it, nourish it. Dress it up for an amazing girl's night or a hot date. Focus on taking care of you and owning that fact that there is only one of you in life. We're all doing the best we can in this perfectly imperfect thing called life. When those feelings of self-hate come into play just remember you are worthy, you are strong, and you are loved. Always.

KEY TAKEAWAY
Nikki King

@nikkikingfit
@momfidentaf
#selflove club

CHAPTER ELEVEN

Courtney Gackstetter

Courtney Gackstetter is a certified Life Coach and owner of Jane and Thunder, an all natural and allergen free personal care product company designed for mamas and babes. She is passionate about life, natural health and helping women live holistically healthy lives. She lives in the Toronto area with her hunky hubby, three precious children and occasional foster dog. Courtney spent her early years acting in theatre, film and performing live comedy. She since has worked in natural cosmetics/health educating, training and formulating products for well known cosmetic and health brands; later starting her own beloved brand Jane and Thunder, the first natural allergy free cosmetic company.

Find Courtney:
@janeandthunder | @mrs.courtneyjane |
www.janeandthunder.com
Author Photo: Kristen Recalis Photography

"You are altogether beautiful, my darling, beautiful in every way." — Song of Solomon 4:7

The story I'm about to tell you isn't a pleasant story, but it's a part of my life. It's my story. It hurts to write it and it might sting you a little to read it. My hope in sharing this with you is that you can find freedom in your own story. To discover what truth is, and to break free from the lies that we have believed to have been true that have been spoken over us intentionally or unintentionally.

This is the story of the first time I believed the awful and disgusting lie that my weight and appearance are attached to my self-worth. While I'm going to share it, and it involves quite a negative picture of my father, I want to try to be as forthcoming and honest, while still honouring him as my dad. Although, to be honest, I am really struggling with how to tell this story while honouring him. I'm going to try my best, so please bear with me. Allow me to start by being clear:

Has my dad been a great father? No.

Do I have daddy issues? Yes.

Do I want to speak ill of him and how he's treated my family and me? Absolutely not.

Do I pray for him and wish him well? Yes.

I actually haven't seen my father now for half my lifetime.

Going through inner healing and prayer, I realized this story had really shaped and painted my internal dialogue for a long time. I realized that my false self-worth was actually rooted in my father's brokenness.

It was a special day, because my family and I were all out together grocery shopping. It was a rare thing for all four of us to be together and some of my most favourite memories are of us all together as a family. My dad was a firefighter, so he was either at work, sleeping because of shift work, or out working on his company doing roofing and skylights. So I truly was cherishing this day of grocery shopping.

I was six years old, sitting in the back seat of our very '90s grey sedan (not in a booster seat because what were those back then?) Beside me was my brother, who was seven years old, my dad driving up front and my beautiful mom in the passenger seat. We were sitting in a grocery store parking lot when my dad suddenly exclaimed, "Look at that whale!" His tone was rather disgusted, but as a six year old, I was excited and confused as to where this whale was. There was no water around our suburban Ajax 'No Frills' parking lot, so I was searching for the whale thinking, *maybe it's a cool sticker on a van nearby!*

My mom scoffed at my dad under her breath, "Ian!" while trying to remain quiet and clearly upset that my brother and I might catch on. All of this happened really fast, and it wasn't until I looked at my dad and saw he had been pointing at a woman walking by with her grocery cart.

My still confused six-year-old mind knew my dad was

being mean, but I didn't understand. She wasn't that big? Certainly not a whale? Why had he pointed her out at all? Why is he so disgusted by this seemingly sweet woman, probably a mom, just buying groceries for her family?

What happens next is something a six–year-old daughter cannot forget her daddy saying to her mother. My dad turned to my mom, still with disgust in his eyes and voice. "If you ever get fat, I am leaving you," he threatened.

Wow. I have to stop and take that memory in for a moment, before I release it and let it go. My mom I think was in shock. I know we all were, but that painted a new reality for me...

Surely, Courtney, know this, if YOU ever get fat, your daddy will leave you...

Children internalize almost everything. Our brains are growing so extremely fast, our reality can easily mix in with the developments of our memories, emotions, and thoughts. We're learning so fast that things sometimes get jumbled together. Things we learn and hear from our caregivers, the ones who are there to raise and protect us, become our gods in a sense. They are the ultimate in truth, knowledge, and strength. Small children do NOT always know that their parents can be wrong.

I mean, how many times do you hear little kids fighting over whose dad is better?

"I have the best dad!"

"No, I do!"

"Yeah, well, my dad is stronger!"

"Yeah, well, mine can yodal!"

We look up to these imperfect parents of ours and don't understand that if they are broken, we internalize it as we the children are the problem. So I took this lesson, not wanting to be abandoned, and I kept it hidden in a dark place in my heart. That lie should never have been there in the first place, but it continued to grow as I started adding new lies as foundational beliefs due to my father's brokenness.

Fast forward two years, when I'm eight years old. I am sitting on the couch after school, watching TV with my dad. I was having a wonderful time because in my mind, all is right with the world. My daddy is home! He was my "safe" place and I was his little girl. He looked at me with that disgusted look and tone in his voice I remember from a couple of years ago and says, "Courtney! Stop eating chips you're going to get fat!"

Oh, the shame that washed over me all over again was instant. All I could think was: *I know what that means, that means you won't want me anymore and you will leave me.* I was suddenly so embarrassed to be holding that bag of chips. I tried so quietly to close the bag, but I didn't want to bring on any more attention. I wished I never touched that bag. I saw it as a very bad enemy. It had the power to render me unwanted, unloveable, and unworthy. It could make me fat and that means my daddy will leave me. I folded up the chips and never went for them again.

Another early memory I have is of my mom looking at

herself in a home video. She was clearly embarrassed and commented, "Oh, Lord, my butt is so big! How awful! I need to go on a diet. Is my butt really that big?" She would also do this while looking at herself in the mirror. Are you catching on? Do you know what this taught me? Not that my mom thinks she has a big butt. It taught me that I'm supposed to look in the mirror and find what's wrong with me too. To me, my mom was perfect! She is my idea of beauty and there is no one more beautiful to me than my mom. Truly! Do you know that Teresa Barbie doll was my favourite Barbie? Why? Because she looked like my mom! Do you know that one of my favourite things to bring to school or have as a snack were the tiny red-boxed raisins because the picture of the pretty lady with the long curly hair looks JUST LIKE MY MOM? She was and is still the most beautiful person! She taught me what beauty is and to me, it wasn't possible for anyone to be more beautiful than my mommy!

So hearing this from the most beautiful, important woman on the face of the earth unfortunately set up a self-narrative for myself that I, too, must have things wrong with me. I, too, must be too big in some areas. And if I was too big, I would be unwanted. My mother was not ill meaning like my father had been. What she said wasn't intentional. She didn't want me to pick myself apart as well, and if she had known that I would internalize anything she said about her body, you bet she would have ONLY sung herself praises in hopes that I would too.

Does any of this sound familiar?

I started struggling with my weight and noticing it in third grade. That's when I started having to wear a bra. Yes, I was eight years old when I *needed* a bra. I remember my mom ever so gently telling me that I was going to start wearing a bra and we needed to go shopping for one. She said that I was growing up fast and that she was proud of me. Bless my momma's heart for trying to make it something not to be ashamed of. After my mom and I searched for a while, desperately trying to find something that would fit my child-sized frame, I settled on cotton sports bras. I was so just annoyed by all of this, and it was not as fun as I had hoped, (I mean, c'mon I was eight!) and now the new reality of having to wear one every day was just more work and effort. This amounted to a totally annoyed eight year old, whom I'm SURE had to be kindly reminded daily to put it on so that I wouldn't be embarrassed if someone saw through my shirt.

As you might guess, even though it took a while to truly recognize that my chest was growing, the shame quickly entered. A part of my body was getting bigger, and "gaining weight". What if my dad noticed? How do I hide them? Should I be ashamed of them?

Isn't it both incredible and heart breaking how innocently children connect the dots? We tend to tie things together at such a fast pace because we are learning at a genius, accelerated pace. From the time we are born to eight years old is our 'genius zone'. This is why little kids whom are bilingual can learn languages so fast. However, it's also the time when our core beliefs are formed and forged, thus making it harder to undo lies and false beliefs. This is why so many key moments that have shaped us in our life, whether good or bad, are from our early childhood and quite often in our subconscious beliefs, which are harder to identify. Lord have mercy!

Alright now, back to my boobs.

For all of my single life, I struggled with hating my breasts. I found them to be in the way of sports. Finding clothes, bras, and bathing suits that fit was always frustrating. My ballet teachers used to get upset with me because I was the only girl that had to wear a bra with my leotard as the built-in bras in the leotard were a joke. I spent so many years being frustrated and wishing my breasts were smaller, trying to hide them, and using duct tape so I could zip up dresses. I wore two sports bras during gym so that I didn't get black eyes. Where did I learn and believe I needed to hate them? What emotions strike up? FEAR. Fear of being not wanted because my dad told my mom he would leave her if she got fat and he told me I was starting to get fat!

Did my dad ever bring up my breasts or look at my growing womanly body? No! Not in the slightest. But those were the false beliefs I had tied together in my mind as a child and continued to carry it with me into my adulthood. I felt shame over my breast size and I carried a fear of not being wanted or not being good enough if I got 'fat'.

I remember in second grade, one of my friends asked our teacher randomly: "What are your boobs made out of?" Innocently so, she responded with "Fat. Your boobs are made of fat." It's easy to see where my eight-year-old brain made connections and what connections were made. Fat = bad. Boobs are bad.

Now here's the redemptive part of my story surrounding my 'tatas'. When I got married, my husband was ecstatic with my body. At first I thought he was lying (*obviously*), saying how beautiful I was. I didn't believe his enthusiasm in the slightest. I had made up so many lies about how imperfect my body was, and I didn't realize that was only according to *me*! I had felt like I was supposed to be ashamed of my breasts, they were too big (according to me), meant to be hidden (according to me) and overall a burden. All of these false beliefs I had bestowed upon my bosoms. So when I learned truly how much he delighted in them, it was truly a relief.

"You mean, they aren't gross? You don't think they're too big?" I asked him.

"What? No! They are perfect!"

I was shocked and relieved.

Insert more redemption when I became a mama for the first time and I was able to breastfeed my baby. Now, suddenly, my lovely lady lumps were life-giving, necessary, needed, and a source of comfort to my precious babes. Wow! What a huge (pun intended) gift I had been given with my jolly joy-making jugs. Seeing the reality and facts that my milk-makers brought life and goodness to my loved ones really smashed my false beliefs I had wrongfully stored up over the years. They weren't imperfect or a burden at all. Instead, the opposite was true. They were a life giving gift. Now I can truly say my beliefs have changed and I do not struggle at all in this area but, instead, am able to delight with gratitude in the womanly gift they are.

So how do we re-write the narratives, the lies, that have been ever so ingrained and learned by us at such a young age? One of the first things is to search and recognize your TRUTHS. How can we make sure as women, we speak truth and a beautiful healthy narrative over ourselves, our daughters, and our sons? I believe that the answer is to start with ourselves. Our internal dialogue is so important. I can bet that if one of your children had some of the negative internal dialogue that you have experienced yourself, it would absolutely break and devastate your heart. Why? Because you're a great mom and it pains you to see your child believe anything that is not the truth about their self-worth. You know who they are created to be and who they are made to be and that they themselves are created *on* purpose *with* a purpose. And mama, don't you know the same is true about YOU? How do you think your heavenly Father feels when he hears his daughter talk negatively about herself? Don't you know that you were made on purpose, made in the Image of God, the creator of the universe, and that you are beautiful, you are His masterpiece? A big part of self-love and self-worth is recognizing this truth about how perfectly you were created. God makes no mistakes, ever.

Self-love, *radical* self-love, is also doing the hard and deep work of removing mould, dirt, and all the other nasty things in your life that can be from your past and that are often lies. If your foundation is built on lies and beliefs that your worth and lovability is based on conditions other than just BEING, girl we have some deep uplifting to do.

Here's a meditation and prayer exercise I find helpful that I have learned through counselling and coaching. If you would like to read through it, I promise it will help begin uprooting the lies and beliefs that have ever been spoken over you. (Forewarning, it can be quite intense!)

For me personally, I have a faith in Jesus; He is my Heavenly Father and whom I owe all to. I picture him showing me past memories as I'm comforted by Him. If that isn't your jam, or your jam yet—don't worry! I will always recommend asking for His help, but you can totally ask the creator of the universe to help guide you through this meditation. Another method used in counselling: go back into your memories, especially any painful memories, and picture your current adult self helping and comforting your younger self at the age of whatever memory you are brought back to.

Ah! Deep stuff. Are you ready?

**Also I need to note, if this is too painful or brings up memories you weren't prepared for, please seek professional counselling and help! MENTAL HEALTH IS SELF-LOVE.*

Prayer/Meditation for Self-Love:

"Creator of the universe, when did I first believe the lie that.... [INSERT HERE]"

"Can you please show me so we can get rid of it together?"

Recognize it and picture Jesus, God or yourself there comforting your child self.

"Where were you in this situation, Jesus?" and often you'll see Him appear.

Say thank you and receive comfort for the child within you. Now, we need to repent and rid ourselves of that lie and replace it with truth.

After I complete the above prayer, I often ask myself a few questions to journal. Try these if you want to test your self-love skills alongside your prayer/meditation:

What memories came up for me today?

What lies do I need to let go of?

What do I need to ask forgiveness for, or repent, that doesn't line up with God's truth about me?

What are the new truths and mantras I can repeat when I feel this lie creeping its way back in?

Is there anything I need to forgive myself for?

We are not our bodies; we are not what other people think of us, or expect of us. We can break free from the limiting beliefs we tell ourselves, whether they were created inside of us or learned through observation or other external sources. We are so much more that all of that.

I am truly honoured to have walked through this with you. I pray that in sharing my story with you, it has enabled you to open up more with the one who loves you most. The Creator of the Universe. He loves you and thinks you are so worthy of love and life and dying for. You were made on purpose with a purpose and when He made you, He made no mistakes, none. You are beautiful.

I'd love to hear from you. Please let me know if any of this has touched you. I am a freedom fighter and if you too have gained some more freedom in your self-love journey, please let me know and let's be friends.

Blessings, always.

KEY TAKEAWAY

Courtney Gackstetter

@janeandthunder | @mrs.courtneyjane
@momfidentaf
#selfloveclub

CHAPTER TWELVE

Adriana Wilkin

Adriana Wilkin is a proud elementary school teacher and photographer living in Clarington, Ontario with her husband and two amazing children. In her early years, Adriana was a Fitness Instructor and had a small bootcamp business. She loved motivating and inspiring others to lead an active and healthy lifestyle. More recently, she has started a lifestyle family photography business where she is fortunate to be able to capture special moments and milestones for couples and families. Adriana is passionate about helping women look and feel their best and inspiring women to love themselves fully. Most importantly, she strives to be a strong role model for her daughter and son. Adriana is an avid reader and writer and a self-proclaimed "foodie" and family chef.
In her free time, she enjoys dancing around the house with her family, doing yoga, drinking tea, and watching television with her husband.

Find Adriana:
@adrianawilkinphotography

You know when you're uncomfortable with something so you keep looking away? You try to ignore this big, uncomfortable thing like the plague. You pretend it doesn't exist; you essentially go into denial about it and things around it, just so you don't have to face it. We don't like to face things that make us uncomfortable. Why would we? Other feelings are bound to emerge such as sadness, hatred, and maybe even disgust. As a defence mechanism, you shield your eyes, look down and push that uncomfortable thing way into the back of your mind where you don't have to see it or think about it. That is how I felt about my body.

Wow, just writing that was tough and reading it back is a struggle, but believing it is almost impossible. Except for the fact that it *is* possible; it was true. Here's the thing....it's extremely hard to look in the mirror and face things that you don't like physically, but it is another thing to challenge who you are as a person. Luckily, I was able (over a very long period of time, might I add) to use this as a point of growth, acceptance and eventually love.

You see, growing up, it felt as though I had it all. I was fit, athletic, happy and healthy. I would go to the gym twice a day sometimes because I was bored. (HA! Writing this as a mom now actually makes me laugh out loud. Imagine being bored?) I have always been such a positive and optimistic person. What can I say? I love my life and always have! I had amazing self-esteem (thanks for always boosting me up, Mom!) and I worked hard to achieve every one of my goals! I became a fitness instructor and started to run my own Bootcamp classes, and then I graduated university and got my dream job as an elementary school teacher. I married an incredible man and we had two beautiful babies together. Wow! Somewhere in this happiness, in the best moments of my life when I loved harder than ever before, I forgot to love myself. That's a powerful realization, isn't it? I don't even think that it was something that I had noticed at the time, but looking back now, I can see the disconnect. I see when I went from being a fun-loving girl to a hard working Mom. I didn't treat myself right, in fact I didn't treat myself at all. I was a Mom now...a role I had wanted since I was four years old. During this incredible time, I forgot to look in the mirror; I forgot to put on lotion after a shower; I forgot to move my body every day; I forgot to take time to do things that I enjoy doing; I forgot to love myself. As if that wasn't bad enough, I developed an angry and depressing internal dialogue. Although I was proud of being an amazing mother, I wasn't kind to myself in any other way.

In my opinion, a lot of women associate self-love with loving their physical appearance, but there can (and should) be love even when you are in a season of change. After having my first child, I most definitely wasn't excited to hop in front of a mirror, but as I said before: deflect and ignore. Instead of owning my postpartum body, I went into hiding. My internal dialogue that I built up subconsciously did so much damage that it was almost irreversible. Every time I walked past a mirror, I would grunt, "ugh!" Every time I stepped on the scale, I would blow out a long breath and shake my head in disappointment. Every time I would see a picture of myself, I would speak with so much hate: "Ew! Delete that! I look humungous." I thought that my problem was with my body. I thought that if I could just be thinner like I used to be, then I would love myself again and I would be happy. But here's the thing: I was freaking happy. Being a Mother has truly made me the happiest that I have ever been in my life. Turns out, that it wasn't happiness that I was seeking and it wasn't a fit body (although losing baby weight a little quicker wouldn't have hurt), it was love and grace. Honestly, I didn't treat myself with kindness anymore. I didn't take care of myself, I didn't go out and do things that I enjoyed doing. I know a lot of moms can relate. Heck, it was tough when my daughter was born; imagine how much time I had for myself after my son arrived 18 months later! I had totally forgotten to love myself. I loved my babies. I loved my husband. I loved my family. I loved my friends… but I didn't take the time to love ME.

I used to want to hide myself in public, always afraid of seeing people that I knew, especially people from the past. Being a mother has made me the happiest and the proudest that I have ever been in my life, but it has also made me the most fearful of others' judgements. This fear, I have learned, goes away with self-love. Positive self-talk, acceptance and love are really what helped me to overcome this fear. Even though it can sometimes still be a struggle, I realize how common this is and remind myself that I don't know what problems that the other person is facing as well. So, I've learned that the best thing to do is put on a smile and be kind to myself and to whomever I encounter. Unfortunately, there will always be haters. When I am fearful of others' judgments, I just remind myself that their issue (or non-issue) with me is *their* problem and not *mine*. Judgmental jerks will be judgmental jerks. It doesn't matter what you look like, what you have accomplished in life or who you are. So let them be. Loving yourself is all that matters at the end of the day.

I get how horrible it feels when you don't look the way that you want to. I have felt the struggle of looking in the mirror and being disappointed. But I wanted to challenge this mindset. First, why do I define my self-worth by my body? Why does my weight or size or shape determine my happiness? If that's the case, then I'm going to struggle a lot in this life. I am surely going to go through phases where my body is going to be bigger, smaller, stronger, weaker, and even pregnant! It's time for me to start accepting that there will be changes and seasons and that they are okay. I've always been extremely health conscious. I've focused on eating well and exercising in order to live an optimal life. Happiness, health and longevity have always been the goal. To combat the feelings of sadness and frustration that

I felt when looking in the mirror, I decided that I would focus on eating healthier, more nourishing meals and being more active every day. Did I lose ten pounds in a week? No. Did I feel better about myself? Absolutely! I didn't like where I was, so I decided to move. If you're finding yourself stuck like me, then try changing it up and do something differently. You are not a tree! I am not a tree! That has been my mantra. I am not stuck and it is such a helpful reminder. Even moving for twenty minutes a day has not only been a crucial part of self-care, but made me feel great, which, in turn, helped me to love myself more. I felt stronger and energized and it is wonders what a little bit of exercise can do for anxiety. When life feels heavy and I feel stuck, this is my go-to. I don't worry about quick change, or becoming a different person. I love myself and trust that this phase will pass. I go back to the basics of exercising, eating real foods, meditating, reading, and spending quality time with friends and family. It is incredible what loving yourself can do for healing. The elephant hops off your chest and you can breathe deep breaths again. I close my eyes and say "I love you," then I tell my husband and children that I love them. Then I put in the work.

I am not defined by my weaknesses and my body image. My self-worth is not determined by how many rolls my stomach has when I sit down or when the extra fat on my arms shake when I wave. I freaking love myself, no matter what season of life I am in. I love myself unconditionally.

Let me say it again for the people in the back: I LOVE MYSELF UNCONDITIONALLY.

Is it hard to share this? Yes. It is so, so hard. But transparency is key. I know that I am not the only woman out there who needs to prioritize themselves. I know that I'm not the only woman who could use a little more self-care and a lot more self-love. That is what fuels me to share my story and the lessons that I have learned. I have always liked the person that I am but all of the negative self-talk over my body image was really bringing me down. Admittedly, I started second guessing myself as a person, who I was and what I stand for. Horrible thoughts would enter my mind like *you used to be a fitness trainer and now you're fat. How do you call yourself a healthy person when you look like this? Everybody thinks you're lazy. How come everybody else can lose the baby weight quicker than you? You are not who you used to be and don't try to be, you'll just embarrass yourself.*

Admitting this gives me a pain in my chest and makes tears well up my eyes. But, it's the truth. Fears and negative self-image can be so limiting. If you can relate to me then I'm sorry that you have thought those things about yourself. I'm incredibly sorry that I have thought those horrible things because as it turns out....I'm freaking awesome. And I'm willing to bet that you are, too! My flaws exist and sometimes they are more obvious than I would like them to be. But those flaws don't hold me back any more. I can still be a fitness and health enthusiast without having a body ready for a fitness competition. I can still be a good mom that rolls around on the floor with her kids without being a size 2 or 6 (or 10 or 22!). I can still be my awesome self! I embrace the things I don't like about my body the way that I embrace the things I do like. I am controlling and I have cellulite, cool! I am a procrastinator and my skin still breaks out with acne, c'est la vie! I am a lazy perfectionist and I have a ton of awesome photos of myself with a double chin, oh well!

In my experience, one seemingly dark hole that is so hard to climb out of it once you have fallen into, is comparison. It is a huge struggle of mine especially with social media and all of the seemingly "perfect" people that we are exposed to on a day to day basis. It is so hard not to be jealous, envious or feel like crap when I compare myself to others. When my daughter was born, I decided to take her to the mall. She was only a couple months old and I thought it would be a great opportunity to get out of the house and go for a walk. I had on my yoga pants and my hair in a messy bun, but I was free of spit up, my face was moisturized and I'll be damned if my daughter didn't look adorable. I had to drive twenty minutes to get to the mall and I'd be lying if I said I didn't feel like a walking hashtag: #killingit #momlife #outwithmybestie! I felt so great, confident, and happy. Then, I saw her. I literally stopped in my tracks. A mother of a toddler and a newborn baby (and this baby was fresh, let me tell you). This momma had her hair curled, an adorable, chic outfit on, a face full of gorgeous make up, and not one but two quiet and adorable babies just chillin' in their stroller. This momma did not look as if she had any children let alone a newborn; she was teeny tiny and looked ready to walk down a runway. I thought that I was winning at life but my triumph fell flat when I saw this woman and compared myself to her story. The dark hole of comparison tried to suck me in. But I said to myself, *no, you don't!* I looked at that mom (and silently) said *get it, girl!* I found myself saluting this mom, because she seemed to have it all. It truly was a remarkable sight but it **didn't mean that my outing was any less remarkable**.

I started thinking to myself that if I can love my husband, my children, my family and my friends SO fiercely then why can't I love myself the same way, regardless of the circumstances? It is natural to be hard on yourself (very natural for me) but I like to think that that can be a good thing as long as it comes with a ton of love as well.

So, why do I love myself? I'll share some reasons and see if they resonate with you: I love my body because it carried and laboured and birthed two beautiful babies. I love my body because it gets up in the morning when it is exhausted and under rested and when it has been up all night working to feed my baby and it somehow still functions and moves. I love my body because it is strong and allows me to test its limits. I love my body because it allows me to hold two babies all day long and it never gives up on me. I love my body because it lets me move and (in this season of life) abuse it.

I love my brain because it is always thinking about how to create a better life for my family. I love my brain because it organizes every second of every day and keeps our family moving forward. I love my brain because it allows me to not only teach my children but the amazing little kids that I get to work with. I love my brain because it allowed me to go through five years of post-secondary school and to continue learning, growing and evolving as a mother, wife, educator, fitness enthusiast, writer and reader.

I love my soul because it's kind and sometimes a little shy. I love my soul because it is good and caring. I love my soul because it puts others before me. I love my soul because it grounds me and reminds me of my purpose as a mother, educator and over all motivator.

I love me.

I highly encourage you to write down the reasons why you love yourself too. It is therapeutic and so uplifting. Being a mom has really changed my life. I have started to see myself and my future so differently. Everything I do now I do for my kids, and I believe in leading by example. Do I want them to grow up being healthy and active? Then it's time to start exercising in front of them. Do I want them to be happy? Then it's time for me to smile more and show more gratitude. Do I want them to be interested in reading and education? That would definitely be a bonus! Then it's time to get those books out, sit with my kids and teach them. It is natural for your children to want to copy you and that is the driving force behind everything that I do. Sure, no matter how much work you put in they still might not enjoy doing something that you enjoy, but just exposing them to different types of self-love is going to be a great stepping stone for their future. Do I want my children to grow up focusing on what is wrong with them or to critique themselves nonstop? No. It is imperative that I reach for more, that I strive to do better than this. So, I love myself. I love myself openly and honestly and I truly believe that that is the best thing that I can do for them.

We need to be role models for our children. That is my number one motivation in life. I want my kids to see me smile, exercise and eat well because I love myself. This rhetoric has been reversed in our society. I see so many clients, friends and family members who are driven to change themselves through hatred. I can be the first to testify that if you start a diet or an exercise program because you hate your body you will not get anywhere! First, hating the way that you look is horrible and sad. But having such a strong hatred that it is now motivating you is only going to result in poor mental health and self-implosion. This is completely backwards. When I hate the way that I look in the mirror, I actually can't have a successful workout because I'm always just left feeling crappy about myself. It is a vicious cycle. I only move my body when it's out of love. You would be amazed to see the progress (mentally and physically) when you do something good for your body because you love yourself and not because you hate it and are desperate for it to change. When I have thoughts like *you have gained a lot of weight, you look horrible, you need to fix yourself,* it's game over. Instead, I change my mindset. I say *it is harder to do things at this weight, you don't have the energy you used to have, time to take some more time for self-care and self-love.* The former mindset doesn't work. Plus, I want my kids to see me doing things because I love myself! When my daughter says: "Mommy, why are you exercising?" I want to say "because Mommy wants to move her body so that she can feel her best today!" and not "Mommy is fat and wants to lose some weight." So, I love myself first. Even if that means eating salads and working out during the day and finishing off the night with a bag of movie theatre popcorn! Life is about balance, after all! In my opinion, we can never be happy, healthy and full of love when we are constantly critiquing, hating and shaming ourselves for certain decisions that we have made. Life is a balancing act and so is loving yourself. You are bound to go through seasons of change but if you allow yourself some grace during these times you will see that loving yourself through it all can make these moments feel so much better. After all, who is going to have your back if you can't have your own? You can't solely rely on other people's love for you (though it may be beautiful and fulfilling). You have to love yourself, too.

Sometimes, I stop and think that I wish I could love myself as much as my kids love me. They don't see any of the negative things that I see. They just see their mom: a strong, loving, caring, nurturing mom. When I wear my hair down or change my outfit my daughter always says "Wow, Momma! You look beautiful." I melt. I wish I could see myself through their eyes. Additionally, I wish I could love myself like my daughter loves herself. Because let me tell you, she FEELS herself. She's always checking herself out in the mirror, smiling and making faces. She even kisses herself in the mirror. Now that's love! So, I'm going to sing at the top of my lungs (regardless of the fact that I am not technically good) and I'm going to throw a dance party every day because it makes me feel happy and, for me, it's an expression of self-love.

Imagine if we took all of that energy that we spent telling ourselves that we aren't enough or focusing on things that we dislike about ourselves and used it to lift ourselves up. Compliment yourself, do things that make you happy, smile at yourself when you look in the mirror. All of that energy towards love is bound to make a huge difference.

I heard on the radio today that Drake bought himself a diamond ring in the shape of a heart and it cost over $600,000. The radio host said, "Isn't that an amazing form of self-love?" My first thought was *damn, I need to start buying myself more diamond rings* (figuratively speaking of course – I don't want to freak out my husband). So I started thinking about what my diamond ring would look like, maybe it would be worth it to think about yours too. You might be thinking: who am I to be telling this story? Who am I to give advice? Well, I'm just like you: a dedicated mom who works her butt off for her family, a woman with good and bad days, ups and down (and you can't forget about those hormones!). I am winning and failing every day. Some days I am full of self-love and other days I struggle. I am constantly finding ways to better myself for my family and to live an enjoyable life. I have been working so hard towards self-love and development. I've lived through seasons when I've looked in the mirror and thought *damn, girl!* I've also been in seasons when I look in the mirror saying the same thing with a completely different context. I have felt disgusted in myself and I am ashamed of that. I'm a mom who can only hope that her kids don't have the same struggles. I pray that they love themselves unconditionally, as I am learning to.

I no longer want to hide from myself in the mirror. I no longer think those horrible and nasty thoughts that used to consume me. I spend more time thinking about growth and development rather than reliving the past and regretting certain decisions. I treat myself graciously and empathetically and most importantly, lovingly. I am thankful to have an amazing support system to help lift me up when I'm down and to make me smile bigger when I didn't think that it was possible. I'm grateful for the love that my family shows me and the love that I show myself.

So, ladies, look in the mirror and give yourself a kiss. Let's love ourselves! We deserve it and we are so worth it.

KEY TAKEAWAY
Adriana Wilkin

@adrianawilkinphotography
@momfidentaf
#selfloveclub

CHAPTER THIRTEEN

Megan Shipp

Megan Shipp might live in small town Rocanville, Saskatchewan, but she hasn't used that as an excuse to stop her from reaching some big goals in her life. Megan has been Executive Director of an Early Learning Centre, writes a regular happiness blog, and is currently raising three amazing littles of her own. Her most amazing accomplishment so far might be losing 100 pounds and getting her health on the right track. Her training and knowledge on the subject led her to health and wellness coaching. As a result, she has changed the lives of many small town moms, and is now sharing some real and tangible advice about how others can reach their goals no matter what their circumstances.

Find Megan:
@this.moms.wellness

I got engaged when I was twenty. I got married when I was twenty, and I moved four hours away from my family and the only life I had known. I graduated college, but didn't have a job. My husband did, and we were content to be living on love. We bought an acreage close to where my husband worked, in the middle of nowhere. The day we got married my husband had a falling out with his boss (at our wedding reception no less), and he promptly quit his job. I was now married, living away from the life and family I was accustomed to, we had no income, and I now had to live up to the ideal wife profile that I had portrayed in my head. From the moment we left our reception, I said good night to my parents and I started to cry. I continued to cry until I fell asleep. What had I done? *This is where I will start my story.*

When I say that we lived in "the middle of nowhere", I mean that our closest neighbour was a half mile away in Manitoba, and we were in Saskatchewan, Canada. We did not have satellite or cable television, and (no joke!) I *walked* to the neighbour's house, at night, in the dark, in the dead of winter, to use their dial up internet a few times. My adult life appeared to be shaping up as a funny tale that I would one day tell my grandkids. This was not what I thought my life was going to be; I had some choices to make. I could choose to keep crying, to blame other people or to give up and move back home. Or, I could choose the adventure, and use my belief that if I worked hard anything was possible.

I think it's hilarious now to look back on the early stages of our marriage. The glamorous days of my husband working on an oil rig in Alberta; a trial at our own business venture; losing everything and subsequently coming this *close* to claiming bankruptcy by age 25. We brought our sweet baby girl home in the spring of 2007…to a local bed and breakfast…that was only afforded by my husband bartering his physical labour in exchange for our rent. We also spent time living in a one-bedroom hunting shack with our first born where I melted snow to wash my hair. *This is just the tip of the iceberg*. The story of our marriage could be an entire book by itself. My husband and I both went back to college when our daughter was two and each spent two years balancing full-time jobs, a child, a house and going to school two hours away from where we lived. This chapter is a snippet of how I became the woman I am today through all the complex and varied struggles I've worked hard to overcome.

As you can see, my life got messy. With all the "messy-ness" and hardship, I turned to food. My heaviest weight was 275 lbs. I'm 5'6. My brother played college football and is 6'3 and he used to weigh the same amount at his muscular peak as a linebacker. I was not a linebacker, and I'd never played football. There was a time where I would stand in my pantry and stuff handfuls of marshmallows in my mouth. I spent a lot of time crying in my closet. I spent a lot of time alone, angry, bored, and sad. I used food for years to numb how lonely I was living far away from family and friends. I used food when I was stressed while working full time, raising a two-year-old, and going to school full time. I used food when I was tired being up all night with a newborn. I used food when I was bored because we couldn't go out without paying a fortune in babysitters, and there where no grandmas, or aunties, or friends to watch our kids. Food filled all the voids, and it also created many more problems. I was exhausted when I got home from work and just laid still on the couch most nights. I lost interest it going out because I felt uncomfortable in my clothing. I didn't like pictures, I was frustrated, and I wasted money yo-yo-ing between the next great weight loss product and fast food on my lunch breaks.

The woman I am today is so vastly different than the woman I was ten years ago. Or even, six years ago. I weigh 100 pounds less. This is a massive accomplishment. Accomplishing that goal was a four year journey, and it's now become another two year commitment to my health. The person I am now, doesn't want to talk about the weight loss. I am honestly *over it*. It was a thing I did, but I don't think I am special and therefore think anyone can do the same thing if they want to. I guess herein lies the question… Why don't they? From the knowledge I have now, through tears and sweat and hunger pains and spending boat loads of money on the next weight loss wonder program, it seems simple. Clearly achieving a weight of 275 pounds is proof that it is not simple and clear cut. My mom even said to me once during my in-class training: "So how is it...? Is most of it just common sense?"

First of all, I don't believe there is such thing as common sense. Second, if it were such a thing, there wouldn't be a billion dollar diet industry and weight-related illness wouldn't be so high. I am going to share my weight loss story, because it is part of who I am today. When it comes to people "wishing" to obtain some type of fitness goal, I often have very little tolerance for bullshit and people complaining about their circumstances. However, I also have compassion for others because of what I have lived through. Losing 100 pounds is like the miscarriages, broken bones, and screaming matches with my husband. I have understanding and compassion for the overweight person on the bus who chooses to stand, suffering through exhaustion and sore feet, rather than trying to squeeze into the one remaining open seat. I have learned more from my life experiences than reading books and it all is part of who I am today, so I can't leave it out.

The positive people who fill my social media feed stress the importance of being real and honest and loving your body for what it is and what it does. But I don't. Well, I do and I don't. I hesitated talking about my weight loss, because I do not want my weight loss to be what defines me as a woman. It is something I did. A goal I accomplished. A lifestyle I continue to choose to maintain. But it's not *who I am*. I go through times where I ignore the scale, stop tracking, binge chocolate on the couch, stay out late, and drink boozy coffee like it's water. Then I feel uncomfortable and sick and frustrated and angry at myself, and re-focus on the scale (*only because it's a tool that told me when I achieved my goal, and it helps me personally*). I weigh my food, go to bed as early as possible, work out with intentions of hitting my target heart rate zones for 300 minutes a week. There are times I don't go out, because I am focused and want to feel strong and sexy in my body. There are also times when my life is perfectly balanced and choosing healthy food and working out is second nature and easy. As you can imagine, or may have seen on social media, I have lots of loose skin. My midsection frustrates me EVERY. DAMN. DAY. I am frustrated that I gained the weight; I am frustrated that I can't embrace it as freaking fantastic like other women; I am frustrated because my belly button gets infected because of how deep it is and how the skin sags over it. I want to have a tummy tuck and I often think that will change a lot of how I feel. But... having surgery scares me, and the cost is not a priority for my family and our goals. So I live in this body and despite all the mindset tools I use on a regular basis, I still have one area I *hate*. I feel guilty just admitting that. But I think it's important for you to know, if you're reading this and it isn't entirely rainbows and sunshine when it comes to how you feel about your body, that's okay. We are all human, and your feelings about yourself are valid. Nobody has this self-love thing "together" at all times. I worked hard for this life, and in front of our children I talk about how amazing my body is. How amazing it is that it grew healthy babies, how soft it is for cuddling, and how strong I am. The real accomplishment in my eyes is in the person I became through the weight loss process.

My journey to lose the 100 pounds successfully started with the harsh realization that heart and stroke disease runs on both sides of my family. Although I don't smoke or have high blood pressure, genetics play a huge role in heart disease and stroke[5], so I have a high likelihood of developing heart disease, even while living a healthier lifestyle. I have bought and tried EVERY SINGLE weight loss "thing" there is. I *still* see the newest thing and look into it and wonder if it would work, because marketing is just that targeted and sneaky. But that isn't my real life, and I assume it isn't yours either. For me, I needed to learn all I could can about nutrition, and how the body uses food and how it stores fat and gives you energy, and then use that information to learn how to release the uncomfortable body I was living in. After ridding my body of the first sixty pounds, I became a healthy eating and weight loss coach through Canadian Fitness Professionals ("canfitpro"). I already had a great base for how to lose weight, and my curiosity lead me to becoming certified. My plan was to officially know everything I could about how to lose weight and NEVER buy into another weight loss gimmick or program. Completing that certification gave

5 As they do with many other aspects of your life, including your body shape and physical traits that have been handed down through generations. Let that sink in for a minute; you are uniquely you and you are made up of all kinds of inherited genetics. Practice being grateful for that! - Courtney

me new personal connections and the tools to continue to lose weight and not feel hungry all the time. I also gained invaluable knowledge about nutrition that helped me rid myself of the isolating IBS[6] I had been suffering with for the past year. To add to my tool box, I also became a certified personal trainer, all in my quest to create the best life for myself and follow my curiosity. You choose what you buy and bring into your house and then you get to choose what goes into your body. During my journey, there are a few things that helped *me* to accomplish and now maintain my weight loss:

1. Find out if you are an abstainer or a moderator. A moderator is someone who can have one piece of chocolate and then leave the rest for another day. An abstainer is someone who finds it easier to have none of something then some. I realized that I am an abstainer. Most times if there is chocolate in our house I EAT IT ALL! I know that about myself, so I don't keep chocolate in the house. I have to drive to get it if I want it. I have to really want chocolate when it is 9:00pm, -40 degrees, and I have to put a bra on and go out of the house and drive to the store to get it! Learning to control my mindset about food and my relationship with it helped a lot. I love this analogy to explain how easy it is to change your mindset. When I see rat poison, I don't eat it. I don't have to tell myself not to, I just don't. I am not using will power to prevent myself from eating the rat poison. My brain

6 Irritable Bowel Syndrome

knows it doesn't eat that and I can walk away. If you are not a smoker, and someone offers you a cigarette, you don't struggle to turn it down, you just don't take it. That's what you can do with your brain. Rewrite the story you tell yourself about food.

2. I found appropriate alternatives for foods I love. I love cookies, but I can't have them in my house because I have little self-control when it comes to food. So instead, I make a more nutritious, three-ingredient cookie option and my kids love them and I don't care how many they (or I) eat because they are full of fibre and no white sugar. I love pasta, but regularly swap it for a zucchini "noodle" instead of real pasta so I am getting more nutritional benefits and less unnecessary simple carbohydrates. Making swaps for the foods I knew were not ideal to keep in the household was a game changer for me in my journey.

3. I ditched foods labelled "low-fat" and other foods that use buzzword marketing tricks to target people who want to lose weight. Low fat = more sugar. Choosing things that are low-fat will not equal weight loss; just less fat. If you are monitoring your calories, then low fat means less calories, but it usually means more sugar. Having foods that are not stripped of all their fat and sugar are likely more naturally sourced, and the closer to their natural state, the better. 2% yogourt is probably going to have more protein and less sugar compared to a 0% or "sugar free" version of yogourt;

so just because something is low calorie does not make it automatically healthy.

4. Choose more water, more veggies, more fruit, more sleep, more sex, more relaxing, more reading, more adventures, more calm. Think of all the things you get to have more of, instead of focusing on all the things you are supposed to "cut out".

Any sustained healthy weight loss is an awesome accomplishment, but I don't want weight loss to be what defines my life story or anyone else's. It was a thing I did, a goal I accomplished in order to live my best life, because for me, my best life involved being healthy, strong and feeling great every day. My life story is not how I did it or how I maintained it. The story is that there were all the excuses in the world to not accomplish my goals, and I succeeded. If you are looking for why something won't work, you will find it. My story is that because I tried, stumbled, learned, tried again (and again, and again and *again*), I have created a life I am proud of, that I am comfortable in.

Life is complicated, hard, and exhausting. It is also exciting and wondrous and breathtaking and funny. We still live four hours from my family and now have three children and an English bulldog. My husband and I volunteer in our community and both work full time jobs. Just like you, we have bills, and dreams, and are making them a reality with the choices we make daily. Mental health is paramount in my life now. I have lived with bipolar disorder for 20 years. Part of not using food to fill the voids in my life is taking care of my mental health. A sleep-in day for me is 7:00am. I am a morning person and am most productive during that time. By 7:00pm, I am over the day, ready to be left alone and in bed. The mornings are key to my mental health and taking care of myself. Most mornings I wake up between 5-6 am and work out. When my body is sore, my heart is heavy, or there isn't enough space in our family life for me to have alone time, I still wake up before the kids and use the time to read, have a bath, or just be alone in the peace before the day starts.

Self-love is knowing what you need and taking the time to get it. When I am not up before my children my day is a disaster. I need alone time. I work out pretty consistently however it does ebb and flow with life and goals. Caring for my physical body is important to my mind, being physically active reduces stress levels, it improves how I move in the world, how I carry my children, and how I help in my community. There are a few other things I feel strongly about when it comes to caring for mental health and living my best life.

1. **Be thankful.** For everything. This is so important and life changing. I actually walk into my house and say, "I love this house." I actually walk into the different rooms and smile and am grateful for my house. When I am driving and the sun is shining in my eyes, I am thankful for the sun. When my kids are fighting and our house is in chaos, I repeat in my head how thankful I am for my healthy children. Then I am thankful for bedtime and that tomorrow we get to try again.

2. **Look for the good.** Yes, sometimes things are shitty, absolutely. Not all days are rainbows and sunshine, some days just *suck!* But being alive is a gift. Your mindset is a huge part of life. You have a choice for how you view the world and if you choose to see the bad things, the things you believe you are lacking… or if you choose to focus on the good things instead. There is always something good about every day that you wake up alive: sometimes that's it (you know, the being alive part), and that's worth being grateful for! But I'd venture a guess there is even more good in your life than just being alive. Look for it.

3. **Decide.** If you are not happy at your job, either quit or figure out how to be thankful for it. If you dread going to work every day, find something else. If you cannot afford to quit, take courses, or seminars, or an online program while working towards your next job. I was burnt out when we moved to our new town, and despite the qualifications I had to work a different role, I chose to fold laundry, wash floors, and be a receptionist a couple days a week and I was full of joy. I changed how I spent money in order to be happier every day in a job I loved going to that didn't pay as well. Your job is not your life. It's what you do to make money, to impact the world, to share your talents and possibly to help other people. If the job you go to makes other parts of your life suck, because you are frustrated, angry, tired, find a different place to work. If the money is amazing, use that as a reason to be

happy. In our house we say all the time, "My job pays for my epic life." If you are not happy DO NOT take it out on others who work with you. It's your choice to stay, figure out how to be content while there or keep your mouth shut. No one has the right to tear other people down or to make a work environment hostile. That is petty and immature. Quit or change your mindset to make it feel better.

4. **Follow your curiosity.** This one is huge for me. We live hours away from colleges and universities. The amount of activities are limited in small towns for children and adults. We are lucky to live in a time where we can use the internet to research and libraries do still exist. Read everything on a topic that interests you, take online courses, or go to events. When something sparks your curiosity, follow it. It will lead you on a fun adventure, even if it turns out completely different then it started. Whenever I feel stuck with my home life, work life, or physical goals, I follow whatever spark I have. Then I learn something new, or have a new tool in my life

5. **Give back.** Join volunteer boards and better your community. If you wonder why something works (or doesn't work!) the way it does.....find out why. If you don't like how the school does something, join the parent committee and learn why it is done that way, or find a way to change it. I despised back to school shopping; so I joined our school community console, wrote letters, proposed an idea, and for the past three

years, no one in the elementary end of the school has to buy supplies. The school gets them, we send a check, and life is easier. Sitting around gossiping or complaining will not change anything in your life. Be the change you want to see in the world. When something does not work for your life ...chances are it is not working for others. It's a win, win.

Making changes to your life can be overwhelming and hard. Start where you are with what you have. I started with two minutes a day on a recumbent bike. Sometimes two minutes felt like forever; that is where I started with working out and stayed there for a month before I went to five minutes. Small changes do matter. Just start. With the internet there are vast amounts of tools available for free, so start with reading. Find what makes you curious and try it, then tweak it so it fits your life. If waking up early isn't an option because you love to stay up late, then workout at night after the family is in bed, or move your body on your lunch break. Do not wait for tomorrow. Make a different choice the next time you have a choice to make. If you're sad, cry or journal. If you're hungry, eat. If you're tired, go to sleep! You choose your happiness. I think people can get caught up on the things they would have to change, and they freeze-up and don't make changes that are simple and have a huge impact on our lives. Small consistent changes do add up to massive long term results. We get to choose.

Working out can be hard, cooking real food and writing down what you eat can be hard, looking for the good parts of your day can be hard. Living with extra weight is hard, living with inflammation is hard, living with chronic pain is hard, living with stomach pain is hard, and missing out on life events and moments is hard. Choose your hard and own it. If you choose to smoke, don't complain about the cost. If you choose to spend your time scrolling on social media, don't complain that you didn't accomplish your house work, homework, family time, me time, or workout goals. If you don't do the work to have the dream job, don't complain or gossip or tear down the woman who has success because she put in the work.

As I traveled from the newlywed girl, to the lost, obese, frustrated new mom, to the woman I am today, I have spent a lot of time on personal development and I have learned a lot. I took the pieces that resonated in my soul and made me smile and the things that felt.....blah...I left. The greatest gift I have gained is the knowledge that everyone gets to define what their success looks like.

My journey to self-love continues every day. My life is a choice, and making the best choices isn't always easy. Sometimes, I am tired and don't want to work out, or I don't want to go to work or get out of bed. Sometimes, I don't want to talk to anybody or I want to scream at the people I gave birth to, and then I *do*, (and then feel terrible about it afterwards)... I know need to forgive myself for being human. Checking in with myself and doing what is best long term for my wellbeing is the active part of still finding out how to love myself.

You get to make choices and small adjustments to your life, too. Go make your choices and own them and love them and start living a life you love. It's worth it, I promise!

KEY TAKEAWAY

Megan Shipp

@this.moms.wellness
@momfidentaf
#selfloveclub

PART III:

The Path to Finding Yourself

Self-Love Realizations Through Mental Health, Handling Anxiety, Depression, Suicide, Alcoholism and Belonging

CHAPTER FOURTEEN

Jen Mergelas

Jen is a Holistic Self-Care Coach, Fitness Instructor, soon-to-be JOGA Coach and Entrepreneur. She lives in Burlington, Ontario, Canada with her hubby of 16 years and two daughters.

Jen is passionate about empowering other busy Mamas to make time for themselves first. Her 15 years of experience in health, fitness and wellness allow her to authentically coach and mentor her clients to live a wholehearted, holistic lifestyle through self-care.

In May 2019, Jen and her husband Russ launched *Hōl-Lifestyle Inc.* Their company is all about "empowering whole living", provided through fitness coaching, health supplements and wellness events.

Jen enjoys spending time with her family at their cottage in the summer and playing beginner's hockey with her girlfriends in the winter. She loves being a Hockey Mom.

Find Jen:
@jenmergelas I @hollifestyle I @jogajen I Hol-Lifestyle.com
Author Photo: Adriana Wilkin Photography

"Did you get it?" my dad asked for the fourth time this week.

"No, not yet. I'm sure it will come soon," I replied. I couldn't look him in the eye.

We were talking about my report card. What my dad didn't know was that it had been sitting in my desk drawer for a week now, underneath a pile of seemingly random things a teenager would have stashed in her desk. The truth was, I hid my report card because I was afraid to show it to him. Amongst the string of Grade "A" marks, there was a glaringly obvious "C+" in English, my worst subject. And anything less than an "A" was unacceptable. Anything less than an "A" meant I was going to disappoint him, which was something I desperately tried to avoid.

So I was willing to stretch the truth - make changes - do anything to please. In this case, it meant photocopying my report card, cutting out one of the little wee As from another subject, pasting it on top of the English "C+" then re-photocopying it to show my parents my "perfect" grades. (Sorry, Mom and Dad!)

Yes, I felt guilty about this manipulation, but it was quickly overcome by the fact that my now "straight A" report card was going to make Mom and Dad happy and proud. They weren't going to be disappointed in me and they weren't going to scold or criticize me. And THAT was worth all the creative craft work I decided to do.

I've always strived to be the perfect daughter my parents expected me to be. I wanted them to be proud of me, and I was willing to do anything to accomplish this. Little did I know, this pleasing, perfectionist mentality became a way of life for me. I even remember carrying a key chain on my school backpack that said "If you're happy, I'm happy." Making other people happy was all that mattered to me.

I had no idea that loving yourself was even a thing. But my life was good; I was content, since I was able to meet most of my parents' high expectations (...with a little tweaking here and there, of course). My childhood and teenage years were relatively trauma-free, following which I checked all the boxes on their life list to success:

Go to a private high school. Check.

Go to a reputable University. Check.

Get a good job with an important title. Check.

Get married to a successful man. Check.

Buy a big house. Check.

Have first child by the age of 30. Check.

Have another child. Check.

On paper, my life was white-picket-fence perfect. I was living the dream I spent my whole life reaching for. I was pretty much ready to check off the last list item: "Live happily ever after". But then, I realized I was a far cry from living happily ever after. My life, the one that looked so perfect on the outside, was actually quite broken on the inside. It felt like frustration and resentment. Constant anger and sadness. And it was affecting my marriage. The rug that I had been sweeping things under for 16 years was starting to expose its contents. But I didn't want to deal with it. I was terrible at communicating my feelings with my husband and I hated confrontation. So every work day, I filled my schedule with appointments to avoid being home. I continued to sweep my feelings underneath that rug. It was the only thing I knew how to do.

I was riding an emotional roller coaster. During the high periods, I went out with my girlfriends a lot. I drank a ton of wine. During the low periods, I ate poorly, and slept often. But this lifestyle wasn't new to me, so I didn't think anything was wrong. At the time I thought I was just re-living my University years so I could get away from being a mommy and just feel like "myself" again. What I didn't know was that this lifestyle had been a coping mechanism for me for many years. It was how I escaped the unhappiness in my heart. Disguised as Party Jen, I was full of energy, so much fun, and always happy.

Then one random day, I felt the stark opposite of happy. I was driving to work, and suddenly started to cry. It wasn't an oh-my-eyes-are-welling-up kind of cry, but more of a wtf-is-going-on-I-can-barely-breathe bawl. It was like a flood of emotions were literally pouring out of me. I pulled over and continued to cry for what felt like forever. I remember it so vividly that I can actually go back to that moment and relive the sadness that was inside me. Yet to this day, I have no idea what triggered the sobbing. It was like the Universe was telling me, "Okay, Jen, enough is enough. You need to stop hiding." It was in that moment, in my car on the side of the highway, with puffy eyes and a shirt full of tears, that I realized something was wrong. It was only when my breathing settled down, that I realized there was no more room under the rug. I needed to talk to someone. I googled a therapist and booked an appointment the following day.

I went through half a box of Kleenex in my first session. I used up the other half during my second session. Through every word I spoke about my marriage, and eventually my childhood and entire life, the tears flowed. After the third session, and another large pile of used tissues, my therapist said six words that changed my life: "You're showing signs of mild depression." The tears stopped. My eyes widened. I stared at her and said softly, "Really?" It was something I had never considered. I saw my family doctor and at 39 years old, I was diagnosed with severe depression.

Mental health was something we never talked about in our family when I was growing up. To be honest, I don't think we talked about our feelings in general, which is why suppressing them was so natural to me. I was used to putting on a perfect happy face. So when I started to speak to my therapist about the things that were under that rug, my world - and my heart - truly opened up for the first time, with my not-so-happy face. Sharing my feelings was foreign to me, but it felt right. Actually, it was liberating.

It turns out the diagnosis of my mental illness, as difficult as it was to manage at first, was the beginning of my transformation. It didn't happen quickly, or easily. I was put on a low-dose anti-depressant, which helped my symptoms tremendously. I also continued with therapy, and ended up seeing four different therapists in the 8 months that followed my diagnosis.

I know you might thinking, *four* therapists? I used to think therapy was just for really broken people (and as it turns out, I *was* really broken). But I now believe that even the semi-broken and seemingly un-broken can benefit from it[7]. There's just something extremely healing about talking to an unbiased, non-judging person about the good, the bad AND the ugly things in your life. For me, it was like having four lunch dates with four different friends - I would tell my story, and each had different questions to ask and opinions to give. Each had a unique perspective. All allowed me to dig deep and uncover the things I had no idea were important to my self-discovery and healing.

And let me tell you, I dug DEEP during therapy. I thought I was there to fix my marriage, and manage my mental health issues. Instead, I spent countless sessions talking about my past, what my childhood was like, and the years leading up to now. It was only after talking about my life out loud that I learned I had been living only to please others and to be perfect. I realized I had no idea who I really was.

My decisions had never been MY decisions. My choices

7 I couldn't agree with this more. I have recently started therapy and it is life-changing. — Courtney

had never been MY choices.

The things I did? Were to fit in.

The goals I had? Were to please.

This was a tough pill to swallow (no pun intended). After months of therapy I also uncovered that my entire life was spent worrying. I worried that if I did what I really wanted, said how I really felt, or simply just BE who I really was, it might be seen as "wrong". I was scared of being judged. I feared being criticized and rejected. I was afraid of disappointing others.

So I was never truly me. I was always whoever others wanted me to be. I pretended to like things that my husband liked. I never admitted I didn't know about a topic a friend was talking about. I wore clothes that were in-style but didn't like, and listened to music that I hated. I went to places I didn't want to go to. I rarely said "no". I did these things - everything for everyone else - my ENTIRE life.

I let my parents choose my friends, the high school I went to and my ambitions.

My friends chose the restaurants we ate at, the bars we frequented and the clothes I wore.

My husband chose my hobbies, the movies we watched and where we would go on vacation.

And my daughters... well, they ruled my world.

The famous quote, "You can't pour from an empty cup" couldn't have been more fitting. I was running on empty, and I couldn't remember the last time I filled my own cup. Because I didn't know it was a thing. Taking care of myself was something I never thought of doing outside of a mani-pedi. The result? Resentment and frustration, especially towards my parents, and Russ.

It was all beginning to make sense.

This self-awareness was a HUGE step for me. Understanding why I made the choices I had made throughout my life was extremely overwhelming but therapeutic. Analyzing my life was important for me to heal, because it gave me the opportunity to FORGIVE. At first I blamed my parents. How could my Mom and Dad possibly allow me to live my childhood striving for perfection? How dare they force me to go to a private school when I wanted to be with my friends, and brainwash me to dream of becoming a doctor? Then I blamed Russ. How selfish of him to make all the decisions in our relationship! Why didn't he let me do the things I wanted to do?

More therapy sessions allowed me to accept the things I couldn't change from my past. When my therapist helped me recognize that my mom, dad and husband had only been loving me the best way they knew how, I shifted. I shifted from anger to appreciation and understanding. I shifted from blame to forgiveness. It was with forgiveness that I started to shift - slowly - to self-love. Russ wasn't the issue. My parents weren't the issue. I had to take care of ME.

My mental health needed healing beyond a daily pill,

and this was bigger than an imbalance of hormones. It was a 40-year-old WHOLE mindset that needed to change. And a mindset shift is a big deal. It isn't putting more vegetables on your dinner plate or adding 10 minutes to your workout. Mindset work takes time. It takes consistency. It means a whole lot of self-commitment, internal reflection, and behavioural change. And for a people-pleasing perfectionist? I'm not gonna lie, this work was HARD. It still is. But I made the conscious choice to believe in myself and the possibility of living a different life.

I didn't know where to begin at first. Cognitive Behavioural Therapy (CBT) helped somewhat. The resources in general were plentiful – books to help depression, podcasts about self-love, courses about meditation, audiobooks on mental health. I read and listened to them all. It was a little scattered and overwhelming but I felt good about the beginnings of a glow that was on my track to healing and growth.

But then I discovered Brene Brown, and my path lit like wildfire. *The Gifts of Imperfection* book changed my life. I finished it in one sitting, then read it again with a highlighter. I felt like the book was written just for me and my journey.

"How much we know and understand ourselves is critically important, but there is something that is even more essential to living a wholehearted life: **loving ourselves**."
— Brene Brown

In her book, Brene Brown talks about an "unraveling

journey": a time when you feel a desperate pull to live the life you want to live, not the one you're "supposed" to live. The unraveling is a time when you are challenged by the universe to let go of who you think you are supposed to be and to embrace who you are. It was time for me to unravel.

I wanted, so badly, to feel deep in my heart that I was worthy. Regardless of what others were thinking, saying or doing, I wanted to believe that I was enough. And so started my journey towards wholehearted living - to live and love with my whole heart, and accepting myself for who I truly am. I wasn't going to let my past, or my mental illness define me. It was deep, messy work.

I devoured the words of Brene Brown, Rachel Hollis, Tony Robbins, and other personal development gurus. But there was only so much the pages and videos could do to help me heal. I needed to actually DO the work. And truthfully? I would have never done it on my own. I was lucky enough to meet an incredible friend and mentor, and a community of people who were striving for the same thing I wanted - to live the best version of myself, and support others to do the same.

I found inspiration daily. I found motivation and consistency. There is truly something magical about community, and how a group of like-minded individuals can collectively lift you up just by showing up. So that's what I did. Every day for as long as I can remember, I've SHOWED UP. I show up exactly as I am, say what I want to say and do what I want to do. I show up and take care of ME.

My tribe keeps me accountable. My community keeps me consistent. By sharing what they're doing to take care of themselves, I've adopted daily habits that have steered me in the direction of self-love. Every day, they help me feel stronger, more confident and truly accepting of myself. I wish I could promise that if you do the *exact* same things that you, too, can learn to love yourself. But the truth is, the path to self-love isn't clear. It's not a one-size-fits-all journey, and it surely won't be the same for everyone. But what I do know is this: **the path to self-love is self-care**. Take care of yourself first. Move and fuel your body. Feed your mind. Fill your heart. And if you can, do it with others that will encourage, empower and inspire you to keep going strong.

These are my daily non-negotiable activities as part of my self-care routine. Remember that success doesn't come from what you do occasionally, it comes from what you do consistently. Give some (or all) of them a try and see which ones serve you best.

Affirmations - The power of "I AM" used to feel a little woo-woo to me. But I heard so much about affirmations I had to give it a try. I started by writing down one or two affirmations every morning, which eventually grew into seven powerful I AM statements that I now say to myself every day (more on those later). I still feel a little awkward saying them out loud, but I believe there is true magic in impressing these words into our subconscious minds. I also have a beautiful deck of affirmation cards which I pull from daily. I use the card I pull as a bookmark in my planner so I am reconnected and reminded of my I AM statement throughout the day.

Meditation – I used to tell myself that my mind was too busy to meditate. I was the girl lying on the floor during Savasana[8] adding items to her grocery list. Sound familiar? Let's be honest, it isn't called a meditation practice for fun. It takes SERIOUS, consistent practice to get the most out of it. But the more often you do it, the greater the impact. The easier it becomes to find your breath and feel calm. I do a 10-minute meditation every morning, and it's enough to keep me grounded and calm throughout the day.

Gratitude – This was the biggest game changer for my mindset. I write down 3-5 things I am grateful for EVERY SINGLE DAY. It's the little things that make the difference; a big hug you got from your kid in the morning; a warm cup of tea; Indigo blankets (this is often on my list). When you look for things to be grateful for in your every day, you teach yourself how to focus on what's going well in your life, instead of what's going wrong. Gratitude can move mountains when it comes to your mindset, bringing in positivity and happiness, and who doesn't want more of that?

Personal Growth – This is my favourite self-care practice. The truth is, I never used to read books about personal development. Actually, I never used to read. But now? I. Am. Addicted. On top of all the books I already have, I screen shot pictures of books people recommend on social

8 The final pose in many Yoga classes which you generally find while the teacher takes you though meditation.

media to read later. I have a running list of books saved on Amazon, and a pile of personal growth books from the library on my nightstand. Admittedly, I don't read many of them all the way through, but I always take away some key gems. Tony Robbins says, "If you're not growing, you're dying." Find a book and learn something from it. Find a book that inspires you. Find a book that makes you feel like you can conquer the world. Then go do it.

Exercise – Move your body 30 minutes a day. Hit the gym, pick an at-home program, or go for a walk. Just move. The endorphins relieve stress, boost energy and keep your heart strong. But know this: being healthy isn't about strong legs and a six-pack. Being healthy is about feeling powerful in your WHOLE self. I've been a group fitness instructor for 15 years, and I thought I was really healthy when I was teaching 2-3 classes a week. But I can say with confidence that I am the healthiest I have ever been right now - 10 years older and 15 pounds heavier, because I'm not just giving my body love, but my mind and heart too.

I know my self-care practice isn't rocket science, or anything new. I had to try a lot of different things before I found what serves ME best. When I committed to doing these things consistently (like… almost every single day), that's when I really started to feel the shifts. The ripple effect of self-care is self-love and self-confidence. I am now more positive in making my own decisions, more confident in speaking my truth, and more comfortable saying "no".

Taking care of myself carved my path to self-love.

The resentment, frustration and anger has melted away. Gratitude, joy, and love stepped in its place.

I'm sure you know the shift didn't happen overnight. I didn't wake up one morning and think, "I love myself so much!" But I do get up in the morning to practice my morning routine, and feel the shifts all day. It's the little feeling in my heart that genuinely says *I am enough*. It's the sigh in my belly that says I'm going to be ok. It's the pride in my soul that says what I want matters. It's the way I FEEL compared to how I felt before.

And that positivity? That confidence? The peace? Feels pretty darn good.

Now, while these practices have changed my life, the depression and anxiety do still exist. I still struggle with my emotions. I still struggle with my self-esteem and self-worth. And sometimes I still want to just crawl into bed and sleep the day away.

The difference is in my self-awareness. I know what self-sabotage feels like and I know what to do about it. I have tools in my self-care tool kit that can help me manage the little voice that still tells me I'm not good enough. In fact, as I was writing this chapter, imposter syndrome reared its ugly head. Who am I to write in a book? I almost failed English and now I think I can write a whole chapter on my life? I couldn't help but feel like my story wasn't traumatic or interesting enough. Is my story even worth writing? Most readers will probably just skip past my chapter.

Maybe that's true.

But instead of throwing in the towel, I took a few deep breaths and said, "I am brave. I am grateful. I am enough." These are some of the words ingrained in my mind that I turn to when I feel the confidence tables turning. Words that I've been writing down and telling myself every single day for almost 2 years. These "Big 7" affirmations have helped me shift from being a people-pleasing perfectionist to finally feeling comfortable - and completely confident - with who I am, and the story I am telling.

I AM GRATEFUL – I am thankful for all my blessings; for all the little things in my every day.

I AM BRAVE – I have the courage to speak my truth and be authentic. Vulnerability is a gift.

I AM EMPOWERED – I am confident and strong, and my opinion matters. I am proud of my decisions and stand behind my thoughts and beliefs.

I AM LOVED – I receive love with open arms. I am loved beyond measure for who I truly am, not what I do, believe in, or look like.

I AM PERFECTLY IMPERFECT – I love and accept myself as I am, flaws and all. I celebrate my uniqueness and those of others. There is no such thing as perfection.

I AM WHOLEHEARTEDLY ME – I live and love my life with my whole heart, and I am proud to be me.

I AM ENOUGH – I am worthy of it all. I deserve to live the life of my dreams.

I have finally let go of what other people think.[9] I no longer compare myself to others. I don't let anyone tell me what I should do, what I should wear or how I should feel. I've stopped trying so hard to please others.

I do what serves ME best.

Because I come first.

And I want our girls to feel this way, too. I want them to feel loved no matter who they are, or what their grades are on their report card. What sports they play or what they choose to wear. I want our daughters to love themselves unconditionally and take care of themselves first. I want them to feel comfortable speaking up, having an opinion and making a decision. I want them to let go of comparison and be whoever they want to be. And all of this comes from self-care. It comes from self-love. It comes from self-worth. I know they're always watching. They pay attention to how I respond. They are aware of how I handle things in life. They see how I take care of myself. So I keep showing up.

I show up for me. I also show up for them.

I consider my mental illness a gift. It allowed me to uncover who I really am, and feel truly comfortable in my own skin for the first time in my life. It's refreshing and liberating, to finally live MY LIFE. I feel more joyful and grateful, calmer and more grounded. I feel positive, passionate and powerful. I feel like ME.

My days now are so different than they used to be. My

9 A-FREAKING-MEN!!!

days begin for ME, so I can be a better mom, wife, daughter, sister, friend. Not the other way around. By filling my cup very day, I am able to overflow and pour onto everyone else without resentment. By taking care of me first, I can take care of others wholeheartedly. I finally understand the importance of putting on your own oxygen mask first before helping others on the plane.

Self-care is a priority. Self-care matters. Self-care isn't selfish. Self-care is LIFE WORK. LOVE WORK. Wholehearted SOUL WORK.

I didn't tell my parents about my depression and anxiety right away. I was still afraid of judgement and criticism. I didn't want to hear the dreaded, "You have everything, why can't you just be happy?" comment. My mom cried when I told her.

She was extremely loving and supportive. She listened and didn't criticize. Actually, she still checks on me now, to make sure I'm feeling okay. My relationship with mom and dad is so much better because of my journey. I know they have only ever wanted the best for me, which in their minds, was perfection. I understand that now, and appreciate all the love they continue to give me.

And Russ? He is my rock. My biggest supporter, and the love of my life. At first I don't think he understood what all this self-care stuff was doing for me, but he continued to stand by me. Russ has given me more strength than he knows. We have more conversations now, and we work every day to keep our marriage strong. Sometimes, he sends me articles on personal growth and joins me for a yoga class and meditation. The ripple effect is stronger than we think.

Early on in my journey Russ asked, "So, when are you going to be done doing all this self-care stuff?" I was offended at first, assuming he was judging me. Instead, I responded with love and confidence, "Truthfully, babe? Never. I'm going to be taking care of myself for the rest of my life."

And if I was given a C+ for that answer, I wouldn't have cared.

KEY TAKEAWAY

Jen Mergelas

@jenmergelas | @hollifestyle
@momfidentaf
#selfloveclub

CHAPTER FIFTEEN

Carla Goodfellow

Carla Goodfellow is a successful entrepreneur and course creator from rural Southwestern Ontario, Canada. She is passionate about her family, decluttering, home organization… and horses and cats. She believes there is a strong connection between your physical space and mental wellness and her signature course 'Your Lighter Life Blueprint' helps women get started on their decluttering journey through a step-by-step online guide.

Carla is also a Certified Landscape Designer and has grown a successful landscape design/install company with her husband since 1999. But of all her accomplishments, her three children are her pride and joy. Her oldest was born in 2004 and motherhood has been the most motivating reason for finding self-love and happiness.

Find Carla:
@my.lighter.life

"LESS IS MORE."

How many times have you heard that phrase? Have you ever stopped for a minute to appreciate what those words mean when applied to your own life? If you've ever felt like you're not enough, take a minute and recognize that "Less is More" and you are enough now just as you are. You don't need to be more or do more to feel like you matter.

Have you ever felt like you just don't fit in? Like you're different and something in the back of your mind screams, "They don't like you!" That was me. It wasn't that I didn't like myself. In fact, I enjoyed my own company. But when I was around people I always felt inadequate. I never felt like I was interesting enough. Being around people made me feel very anxious and I always clammed up and felt really shy.

That tape played in my head on replay. It played over and over again and kept me feeling small.

"You don't fit in. You're different."

I could share a lot of reasons why I might have felt this way. I spent years speculating and trying to justify these feelings. Maybe it was because I was an only child for nine years? I was used to being alone. Playing by myself and entertaining myself with this vivid, wild imagination. I was the only kid in my small elementary school who could say I had no brothers or sisters and although I took pride in that fact at the time, even at that early age, I felt like I was different.

I could dig deep and tell you all about my teenage years and how I always felt like a disappointment. I never felt like I met my mother's expectations and I always felt like I was in trouble. I had fear of consequences, so every choice I made, weighed heavy. Maybe, it was my own guilty conscience that made me feel like such a disappointment but the emotion was real. It made it very hard to communicate because there was nothing I dreaded more than confrontation. Confrontation opened the opportunity to have someone else's words solidify how I felt inside.

My college years came and I was suddenly around new people. It was a fresh start and I promised myself this was going to be different. How did I decide was the best way to feel comfortable, funny, liked and fun? The party scene and a lot of drinking. I had friends and that was what we did. It took the edge off and made me feel like I could just be me. Whoever that was. I felt accepted. I didn't realize it at the time, but this was the first time I'd used alcohol to cope with my social anxiety. I didn't feel any negative affect during that time but a pattern was established.

I made my way through college, worked for a year and then went back to school. Gratefully, on my return to school, I met my now husband. For the first time, I really felt like I could be myself. We got married, bought and renovated a house together, started a business and at the age of 28, we started our family. We had three kids over eight years and I was happy. I had a great family, a house and a business but as time went on I felt like something was missing. We'd moved to a new community and I wanted to meet some friends.

I started joining different activities and meeting people at events and that underlying feeling started to resurface—that feeling that I wasn't as fun or interesting as the next person and that didn't quite fit in. But I met some really fun friends and loved spending time with them. Weekend BBQ's and get-togethers made me feel like I'd found my place. What I didn't realize was that I was back to using alcohol as my crutch. Using it as a way to find comfort from my social anxiety. Even after all these years, that feeling of being different was still there under the surface and I was still not accepting myself for who I was or believing anyone else would either.

A couple of years later, a new opportunity was presented to me and I thought I'd found the answer. In 2014, I joined an online network marketing company. I actually knew my "upline" well so the promise of friendship and community was enticing. A group of women supporting each other and accepting each other for who they were. It seemed perfect.

I had spent five years prior to this focusing on my health and fitness. I had never really struggled with my body image other than briefly after having babies. In fact, fitness had been instrumental as an outlet for me. I really loved what fitness had done for my self-confidence and how much more energy I had to keep up with how busy mom-life was. This seemed like a great way to meet new friends maybe inspire someone else to get healthy along the way.

It started off great. I felt like fitness was my thing and now I was using it to be a part of something. In the beginning, I felt like I had a little group to check in with daily, friends to share business strategy with but also just chat about life. As I share this next part, I want to be perfectly clear that I do not harbour negative feelings towards anyone I was involved with or with Multi-Level/Network Marketing Companies in general. But for me, being part of this business wasn't healthy mentally and it affected my mindset in a negative way. I truly believe everything we go through is for a reason and I have no regrets. Every experience is instrumental in bringing me to where I am today. If I had never hit my rock bottom and found myself in such a low place, I may never have ended up where I am now: fully loving myself and celebrating my uniqueness and honestly happy!

But to explain further, I need to rewind three years. I wasn't content. I wasn't feeling authentic. I was in the business of health and happiness and I felt like a hypocrite. I was drinking a lot on weekends and I was in limbo trying to figure out who I was showing up as on social media. When I look back now, I realize I didn't really know who I was and it was so easy to compare myself to other women who seemed like they had it all together. I had no clear direction for my life.

THE BEGINNING OF CHANGE

In January of 2018, I had no idea what the year ahead was going to bring. I didn't realize how much I was going to accomplish, nor did I realize the emotional roller coaster I was going to ride. I made a decision that I was committing 100% to a fitness program. That also meant 90 days with no alcohol. It wasn't a 'had-to' decision. It was a decision I chose to make. I had quit drinking three times for pregnancy but never had I given up my social crutch 'just because'. I remember telling myself if I couldn't quit for three months, then maybe that was a problem. Little did I know this was the beginning of a painful and emotional part of my life where I would learn so much about myself.

The year 2018 can be summed up in one word: Loneliness. Even though I had my husband's support and I was showing up as a better mom for my kids, I had never felt so alone in my life. I became a hermit. I didn't message my friends. It was like I was testing them, expecting them to notice this struggle I was going through and wanting them to reach out to me. But they didn't. My social crutch was gone and it was easier to avoid people than try to justify what I was doing.

My inner critic was strong. It told me they didn't want to be around me because I wasn't fun if I wasn't drinking. It told me that they were never really my friends because they didn't reach out to me when I needed them. I sat alone in self-pity. As the weeks went on, I needed to decide what was going to happen at the end of this "sober curious" break. Three months didn't seem like enough to figure things out.

I started reading more personal development books. I read *The Naked Mind* by Annie Grace. She taught me so much about how society views alcohol and how to control my decisions surrounding alcohol. I read, *Girl, Wash Your Face* by Rachel Hollis, who taught me to stop believing the self-limiting stories my inner critic was telling me. I took a good, hard look at who I was and wanted to be. I started to gain clarity.

That March, before my 90-day program was over, I committed to a fitness competition. Not only did I want the physical challenge, I also wanted an excuse to continue my "sober curious" journey. For three more months, I had a reason 'not to drink'. Isn't it interesting that the only drug we feel we need an excuse not to take is alcohol?

I began to feel comfortable attending social engagements. I went to parties, hockey tournaments and even weekends away with friends camping. I learned that I could make a choice and ultimately, no one cared. It was all the stories I was choosing to believe. But in the end of it all, my social circles changed. My friendships changed and I still felt extremely alone. All those years of believing I wasn't enough and here I was alone.

I threw myself into my online-business. What had started a couple years earlier as a fun way to be a part of something took a turn for the worse. When you're at a place in your life where you're feeling really alone, diving in deep to the online world is not the wisest step. I started to compare myself to other women working in the business. I didn't feel successful. I didn't feel valued. I didn't feel important. There was that tape on repeat again, 'You're not good enough'. This was a business of finding 'your people' and building a team. It was crippling and mentally draining. How was someone who had always felt so different from everyone supposed to find 'her people'? Who were my people? Who would choose me? Every day, I put my energy into obsessing over who those people were and how I would show up online to make them want pick me out of all the others who were better than me. I was so focused on comparing my life to everyone else's, trying to be seen as valued, trying to stand out, trying to build a following on social media and feeling like I was falling short. I had lost sight of what I actually wanted from life and had created this false sense of reality based on a device held in my hand more hours of the day than I'd like to admit. Meanwhile, everything else (in my *real* world) was falling apart:

My house was a cluttered, messy disaster. It felt so heavy. There was so much guilt because I knew I wasn't keeping up with my responsibilities.

I was missing out on valuable years spending quality time with my kids. They were growing up before my eyes and I was so focused on finding my worth in this online world and wanting to prove my value.

I wasn't putting effort into my marriage. My husband felt like I didn't care about any of OUR life-goals anymore.

And the worst part was all I'd ever wanted was to fit in and be a part of something and I felt like I wasn't measuring up AT ALL. I was spiralling downward.

FINDING CLARITY

At the time, I couldn't pinpoint exactly why I was bubbling with anxiety and overwhelm. I had this swelling, growing cloud of emptiness and it felt terrible. I felt like had lost connection with everyone. I felt alone again. Really alone.

I needed to get out of my own head. It was time to find happiness within myself. I knew that meant I had to take some time and do some soul searching. I had to make some life changes. I had to refocus and stop looking for outside acceptance to feel fulfilled. I needed to figure out what would bring me joy so I could show up in this world and give back from a positive place. In order to do that, I was going to have to look into my heart and figure out who I really was. I needed to fully accept and love myself and not care what anyone else thought of me. It all hinged on significant questions I had never asked myself before.

Why?

Why did I need to fit in?

Why did I feel like I wasn't enough?

Why did I care what anyone else thought of me?

Why?

I started to gain clarity. I WAS different and I WANTED

to be different. I didn't want to be like anyone else. I wanted my own identity and I wanted to follow my own path. I didn't want to base friendships on feeling like I had to meet someone else's expectations. I didn't want to compete with anyone. I just wanted the mental clutter to be gone. I needed to take a step back from everything and get clear on what I wanted.

I was at a crossroads where I was ready to make a change. For the first time, I realized I could choose how I wanted to view myself and I could change what that critic inside was telling me.

SELF-DISCOVERY

I started on a journey of self-discovery that involved two key components: discovering personality tests and decluttering.

I started to dive deep into personality types. I didn't set out searching for answers about my personality. But when I came across some free online tests, they got my attention. I was so intrigued to find out what these tests had to say about who I was. I thought, maybe, we are all born with personality traits that are part of who we are. Maybe there are parts of us that God created to make us all unique. I wanted to learn more so I could better understand myself and the way I thought. If you have ever taken a Meyers Briggs test or an Enneagram test, you know you can really learn a lot about why you think the way you do and your human design.

What drives us to do the things we do? Why do some people behave differently in the same situation or react with completely different emotions. Our personality types influence how we see and experience the world. One personality type may behave and communicate very differently from another.

I won't go into detail about the specifics of these tests. You can find lots of free tools online. But I'll share a little about what I discovered about myself from taking these online tests.

I am an INFJ (Meyers Briggs test) who is a number 4 (Enneagram test), and these tests revealed so much about how I was designed. It clarified the feelings I'd had my whole life and it made so much sense.

I discovered some of my positive traits: being sensitive to others, being creative, how I enjoy thinking about the deep meaning of life. I value close relationships and am loyal. I learned that the basic desire of a number 4 is to find themselves and their significance and to create an identity. I learned my key motivators are to express myself and my individuality; to create beauty and maintain certain moods and feelings and to take care of my emotional needs before attending to anything else. "Fours" seek meaning and depth in their relationships, their work, or in a quest for personal creativity.

I also discovered how some of the weaknesses of my personality explained so much about why I had struggled with relationships all my life.

Some of my weaknesses include: being overly sensitive and taking everything to heart, having difficulty in opening up and letting people get to know the real me, having high expectations, and getting bored with small talk and wanting conversations to have deeper meaning. When it comes to making decisions, Fours place a huge emphasis on personal feelings rather than objective facts. Fours are feeling-based types who often experience a sense of longing and melancholy. Something is missing for them, which can lead to a quest for wholeness through romantic idealism. When they compare themselves to others, Fours experience feelings of envy.

I had spent my whole life feeling like I was different and trying to 'fit in' when in reality, according to my personality traits, I was created wanting to be fundamentally different than everyone else. I was acutely aware of and focused on my personal differences to the point where I obsessed on the fact that I felt different. After years of feeling misunderstood, it all made sense! I was fighting against my core desire my entire life: TO BE AN INDIVIDUAL!

It was like a switch was turned on and I felt this sense of relief. I could choose to own who I was and justify all the emotions I felt. For the first time in my life, there was this deep realization that I could just be. I didn't need to try and fit in and I could just enjoy each day being me. It really was that simple. The only thing I needed to put my focus on were things that made me feel whole. My happiness was not dependent on anyone else or what they thought of me. It was solely based on how I felt about myself and showing up authentically every day the way God created me.

I am an introvert at heart and I had spent the majority of my life trying to be an extrovert. I always admired people who were outgoing. They seemed so fun. But when I thought back to my childhood and those nine years as an only child, I asked myself: did I long for companionship? Well, not that I could remember. I remember time spent imagining and exploring. Creating and dreaming. Why couldn't my life be like that again? I started to crave simplicity. I started fully embracing who I was and exploring what made me feel fulfilled and what would make my life feel abundant.

The time had come to ruthlessly edit my life.

What did I need to let go of for me to embrace my authentic self and feel self-love to its fullest? Anything that was cluttering my mental space and pulling me back to a place of comparison. Anything that was causing me to feel that I wasn't unique and valid. Anything that was pulling me away from what I valued most. What did I value most? My children, my husband and creating a happy life where I acknowledged how blessed I was every day. Being present and making the most of the time I had with my family. I thought about the future. I did not want to look back one day and realize I wasn't happy and present. I didn't want to live my life always thinking, 'someday I'll be happy'. I wanted that time to be now.

I started to declutter my life.

FINDING MINIMALISM

I stumbled across an article on the benefits of decluttering and how life-changing it could be. What started as a distraction to limit my time on social media, ended up having more impact on my life than I ever could have imagined. I made a choice that I would declutter our home because it had been getting very little attention and a source of a lot of guilt.

Less stuff = Less work = More time.

I wanted our home to feel calm. I wanted my family to know I cared enough to give them a place where they felt they mattered. I thought if I could just get our home back to manageable, I could lose this guilt over one area of my life. I thought if I had less to do, I would have more time to fit in everything I was trying to accomplish. I'd read about the benefits of decluttering and wanted to see if it could apply to me. I started to ruthlessly edit every room in our house. The more I let go of, the easier the space would be to maintain which meant less overwhelm. The less time I needed to maintain and clean, the more time I would have to give to my family. I started making decisions about what we needed and what were just things I held on to. I started to purge. Full-on declutter mode. Anything that didn't serve a purpose in my life, anything I wasn't using on a regular basis or at least for special occasions, was either donated, sold or trashed.

The more I let go, the lighter I felt. After a few weeks

focused on decluttering, I realized how much less time I was spending on social media. It felt good! I wasn't obsessively comparing myself to others. It became clear that every person I had ever tried to feel good enough for didn't matter. I mattered. My family mattered. Why was I spending all this mental energy focusing on people who had no direct impact on my life? The act of removing physical items made me realize I had a choice. I could apply the same tactics I used to declutter the house to the emotional and mental clutter that had built up in my mind for years. I had the choice to let go of feeling like I had to prove myself for someone else. I knew it was time to step away from my online MLM business. I realized it was a source of negative energy for me.

Ultimately, our thoughts and the way we feel about our life has the biggest impact on the outcome of each day. I chose to accept my individuality and the traits that made me me. I chose to start each day being grateful and positive.

My start to minimalism wasn't necessarily because I was spending money I didn't have on things I didn't want. I was spending TIME and mental energy in a way that was fuelling my feelings of inadequacy and I felt my life slipping away.

I was watching my kids grow before my eyes and not being present in their lives.

I felt overwhelmed by the mess of my house.

I felt like I was spinning and couldn't get control.

I felt like I was trying to live other people's expectations rather than actually thinking about what I actually wanted and setting goals that served my purpose.

I was unhappy and did not feel fulfilled.

I was obsessing over what my inner critic told me daily.

It was a vicious, unhealthy cycle and when I found myself feeling stuck, decluttering gave me somewhere to focus positive energy so I could make a lifestyle change I desperately needed. I broke the cycle of negative thinking and silenced that inner critic that was always telling me I wasn't good enough.

I had no idea how much clearing my space was going to make me feel lighter and in control of my thoughts. The process of letting go, allowed me to discover that I could live a happy, abundant life because I was focused on gratitude for all the good things I had in my life.

And that is how 'The Lighter Life Blueprint' was born. I wanted to merge this spiritual freedom I'd found from embracing my unique self with the joy I'd found from decluttering. I wanted to share my experience with others and help them start this process of decluttering. I loved creating and challenging myself and now it was time to use that desire to fulfil my purpose.

I created an online course that successfully launched in January of 2020. It's a course in home decluttering. I truly believe the benefits you experience from simplifying your home, spill into every area of your life. You can find joy and abundance in your life by appreciating the life you have now and letting go of everything you don't need. It's life changing!

LISTENING TO YOUR INNER CRITIC

To find happiness and release mental clutter, I needed to let go of what my inner critic was telling me. That voice inside my head telling me I wasn't enough. But this doesn't happen overnight. You don't let go of feelings you've experienced for years in a snap. Before I could fully let go of these self-limiting beliefs, I learned from what my inner critic was telling me. I took time each day and became intentional with my thinking. I allowed myself to acknowledge that the feelings were real and justified. I also allowed myself to explore why my subconscious told me these stories.

The feelings of guilt, shame, disappointment... I didn't make them up. They were how my human design reacted to my experiences in the world. The childhood memories I experienced impacted the way I viewed myself and how I thought others perceived me. They were valid thoughts that I clung to. A part of my path to happiness was acknowledging those feelings were justified but accepting that it was time to learn and let go. Taking note of what my inner critic was trying to tell me was vital in directing my path. Everything really does happen for a reason. When I listened, I learned to embrace and explore my feelings. I am unique and having a sense of individuality is a driving force for self-love for me. I let my inner critic allow me to believe that my worth was based on the opinions of others, yet it was those very thoughts that guided me to search for my purpose. Leaning into the emotions opened me up to the possibility that I could create my own destiny and set goals that are meaningful to me. When I discovered who I was and that I could love who that was, I found a calmness inside. I didn't have to meet anyone's expectations. I was me. I could love me. I found the inner peace I longed for and I arrived at a new chapter where I could allow myself to love the authentic me.

FINDING WAYS TO MEET MY NEEDS

The decluttering continues. As time passes, things I once wasn't ready to let go of, become insignificant. I let go of old clothes, things I never used, junk taking up space in drawers, those magazines I was saving for a rainy day. I continue to value my time and how I spend it. I keep my social media time monitored and unfollow accounts that start to resurface feelings of inadequacy.

I not only declutter physical things, I set a daily intention to let go of worrying about what people think. I let go of things in my schedule that take my time for things I don't value. I don't feel the need to try to fit in. I accept that when I'm in a room full of people, I can say what is on my mind and not care if anyone agrees with my opinion... OR I can sit in a room and not say anything at all. I can choose to have a drink or not have a drink. I am at peace with who I am. I release the negative thoughts that once played on repeat. All that matters is feeling freedom from the anxiety that crushed my spirit for so many years. I start every day with a simple daily routine. I move my body and take that time to set my intentions for the day. I focus on what I am grateful for. I cherish that I am unique and I start each day with a positive attitude and a full heart.

WHERE DO YOU FIT IN?

As you read my story, I hope it has an impact. If you have ever felt like you're not enough, I am here to tell you that you are. When you wake up in the morning and you feel overwhelmed with negative emotions or you've spent so much time worrying about what other people think that you've lost sight of who you are, know that it's time to let go. Even if you have spent the last 20, 30 or even more years of your life questioning why you don't fit in and comparing yourself, it's never too late to discover who you were created to be. You just need to peel back the layers. Find simplicity. Start letting go of all the clutter surrounding you physically and emotionally and embrace how unique and different you really are. Find joy in that.

The answers are within you. Do some soul searching and find what feels right and what makes you feel fulfilled. You deserve an abundant life. You deserve to be happy! We feel the weight of flaws and failures. We judge ourselves. We compare ourselves. We let our inner critic steal our joy. It's how we choose to move through those feelings that matters. We can choose to let those feelings destroy us and crush our spirit. Or we can choose to use those feelings to guide us on a spiritual journey of self-discovery.

We can choose to keep searching for more. We can choose to believe we need to be more. Or we can open our eyes and embrace that LESS IS MORE! You are enough and everything you need to feel fulfilled and abundant is within you!

KEY TAKEAWAY

Carla Goodfellow

@my.lighter.life
@momfidentaf
#selfloveclub

CHAPTER SIXTEEN

Jennifer Green

Jennifer is an entrepreneur, photographer, speaker and mother residing in Oshawa, Ontario. She has a passion for inspiring and encouraging women to accept themselves as they are and uses her photography to share her own personal journey of self love and discovery. Be You Bou, a boudoir photography business, was created as a way for her to integrate her love for inspiring others while using her art form, photography. Being a mother inspired her to pick up a camera in the first place. She wants her daughter to grow up with the knowledge that she now shares with other women on her platform about self love and worth.

Find Jennifer:
@beyou.bou | www.beyoubou.ca
Author Photo: Lush Photography

My journey of self-love is somewhat like a story. I can clearly see where it all began, the darker side to my journey. It didn't start out from a place of love, but where my journey started is in a way even more important than where I am now. It shaped me as a person and who I am today is because of where I began. Where I am now, I would call my middle; it's lighter at times, which I often confuse with being more relatable. What I have to remember is that one person might relate more to my beginning, while another more to where I am now. But what I've also come to learn with the journey of self-love is, unlike a story, there is no ending.

The beginning of my self-love journey started many years ago and is heavily linked to trauma. It took being where I am now to realize this. If you had asked me a few years ago, I wouldn't have even realized I had gone through trauma. I had spent most of my life numbing it, which held me back from this journey, and from healing. To me, self-love is about learning who you are, embracing who you are and accepting who you are. To truly love yourself you need to be able to forgive yourself for things you might be holding on to. To accept the things you cannot change. To allow yourself grace and compassion. These things aren't always easy but are so worth the work it takes to get there.

I'll be honest, writing my chapter hasn't been easy for

me. I've started so many different versions, leaving trauma out of it due to fear of it being too raw, too dark, writing something that might have been too much to share. I questioned if I should start with my postpartum journey or jump right into where I am now with my boudoir photography business. But nothing I wrote seemed authentic enough and the real origin of my story was missing. As much as I love being a mother and feel so much gratitude towards my business, I needed to start from the beginning.

Wanting to leave out the real and raw stuff, goes to show that I still have a lot of work to do within myself and need to focus on recovering. But I choose to embrace my past because it made me who I am today and I've begun to accept it and maintain focus on my future. Being a boudoir photographer, I get to see acts of self-love from a wide range of women, all at different points in their journey, and that constantly encourages me to push forward in mine. While I'm learning to accept the things I cannot change, I often hold onto shame for the things I have been though. I've come to realize this is okay; it's all part of the healing process. What's not okay is allowing that shame to hold me back from confronting the truth out of fear. I'm working towards letting go of shame to help embrace me more. Here's to the start of that.

Looking back at the girl I was growing up, she's a lot different than the person I am now. I was shy, so very shy that it actually made things like going to school and social events almost intolerable. I was much more of a follower, solely for the fact that I didn't have my own voice. Or rather, I did...

but was too afraid to use it. I spent my entire school years like this and even now struggle with wishing I could change this part of my life. It took trauma to change something I couldn't find the strength to change myself. I found personal growth from one of the darkest times in my life.

I can pinpoint the fear of using my voice, and why I began to change, back to my experience 15 years ago. It took years to make that connection, years of struggling with why this happened, how I could have allowed something like this to happen when it just would have taken speaking up, defending myself and my actions. It also was the start of my co-dependency, the need to fix or heal people to give myself "worth". It's one of those "I wish I knew then what I know now" situations, but I've come to learn I cannot live life wishing, it's now about accepting and making necessary changes to give myself love. It's a work in progress.

The 16-year-old me didn't understand these things though. Heck, 31-year-old me is still learning! I didn't understand manipulation and that there were people in the world that could have it in their heart to use it. I had a very close group of friends, and even though I was very quiet when I was with them, I felt safe to be in their company. I felt safe in my life. I had wishes of being different, looking different, I wanted change… but I felt safe. So, it's funny how trying to save someone else took all that safety away. It tore me away from all I knew and threw me in the middle of something so scary and unknown and without the voice I desperately needed.

A decade ago, the stigma around anxiety, depression and mental illness altogether was very different than what it is today. It wasn't really spoken of, so I bottled up a lot of what was in my mind. I didn't understand why my heart would race and why it would make me feel sick to my stomach. I didn't even know the word anxiety back then. The not knowing or understanding what was going on within my own mind lead to depression and self-harm. The amount of resources that are now available is amazing compared to what was available back then. I am thankful for this now.

At age 16, in the land of good old MSN[10], I was approached by a close friend's boyfriend online, saying he was highly depressed and suicidal. He spoke words that I had only thought in my head and I was, at the time, suffering from depression myself. He used my sympathy as a human being along with my need to help and heal and painted a picture of him taking his own life and linking that with the need for me to see him the next day in the cafeteria to talk about his depression. He told me that no one else would understand, to keep it to myself as it was his story and it wasn't for me to share. The stigma against depression and mental illness as a whole was much different 15 years ago than it is today. So, I listened, I respected his wishes, I respected his depression, and I kept it to myself.

I am, and always will be, there to listen to anyone in need, that part of me has never changed and is a part of me I've always loved. The things that happened next though,

10 HA! Remember MSN? #MEMORYLANE – Courtney

I've spent years wishing could have been done differently. I met him in the café the next day at lunch, I didn't tell any of my friends in order protect him, and I realize now how that might look in the eye of other teenage girls. My need to help and protect someone else then brought me so much hurt and loss.

While speaking to him in person, another friend witnessed a conversation happening and, without knowing the context, assumed that I was trying to steal our friend's boyfriend. What was something so innocent turned into something cruel, and in return, a story which she believed was true. She told her version of the story to the rest of our friends and in that very instant, I lost them all. I lost my safety, all that I had known and suddenly felt like I had nothing. I've always been someone who struggles with confrontation – I close up, shut down and don't perform well. So, while the world was crumbling around me, I shut down.

As I headed back to my locker, I'd felt like I had helped someone just by lending an ear, thinking I had done good and was shocked to find the word, "WHORE" splashed across my locker in permanent marker – felt like a vicious slap to the face. Just seeing that word, I should have known right then and there where this was heading. My heart raced, my cheeks flushed and my voice, which was already so small, was now nonexistent. I was approached by all these girls I thought were my friends, and I hoped they would believe I was a good person, but they didn't see me. Because looking back at that girl, who was so pure and kind yet naïve, I see her. They didn't.

What happened and the events following remind me of those troubled teenage movies you see, where you stop and think Do these things actually happen? Or maybe it happens much more than we know and no one really talks about it as they grow. I know I didn't, I kept it bottled up for years. I still remember the feeling of these girls I trusted, following me home, screaming degrading words at me for everyone around to hear. I had never felt so hurt and humiliated in my life. Being on display for the world to now judge, making people wonder if I really was the person they accused me of being. It did a number on how I viewed myself from that day forward.

One thing I can say I feel blessed about is the fact that social media wasn't a thing in my teenage years. It wasn't until I left high school that Facebook became popular. Had it of been what it is now, I can only imagine the torment I would have felt within my own home, the harassment would not have been saved for school but would have followed me 24/7. It's something that makes me fearful for my daughter. Social media can truly be a blessing and a curse. While social media pushed me head on into this self-love journey, I only hope it can be as impactful in that same positive way for my own child.

I stayed quiet, I didn't fight for myself, and I lost all my friends. Truthfully, I don't blame them. The things we do to protect ourselves and the relationships around us, especially as a teen, I feel that those things don't define us. We take so many factors from sources around us that it's hard to know what is real and what isn't. They believed something that wasn't real and I failed to prove them wrong. What makes a difference is that years later, several of these now women, apologized to me for what happened. Ironically enough, my best friend today is the one who had written on my locker. But from the day she apologized to me, she admitted that she too had learnt and grown so much since then and was wrong – she has never let me down again.

Having already struggled with anxiety and depression, at the time, it felt unbearable having no friends. I had never felt so unheard in my life. I hadn't tried to speak because what would I have said? I felt the need to protect someone's story that was not mine to tell. I had no understanding then that not everyone in the world was a good person. I grew up with a very loving family but was also extremely sheltered. So, there is no way this person who felt comfortable telling me about his sadness could be bad, right? I was wrong.

I was then manipulated into being in a relationship with this person. He told me I was nothing, I had no one, that I needed him. And being with him, what did it matter now? That's what all my friends thought I had originally done anyway. He brought me to such a low point that I started to believe he was right: I was unloved, I was worthless, and he was the only person who wanted me. It was never a relationship and I was able to hold onto things I wasn't ready to give up, for this I am thankful. But it lasted only long enough for him to make me believe that I was loved by him just so he had the power to take it away. He brought back that false sense of safety that I craved only to rip it from me again. What I thought was my lowest point had just gotten lower.

He said I was, "pathetic, a bitch, (that I was) unloved." He actually had the nerve to tell me he did all of this on purpose because he knew I had a kind heart, he knew I would try and help him, and he knew he could ruin my life. I stopped going to school because school felt unbearable. I had never been one to skip school. My grades started slipping when I had always dreamt of succeeding in life. These things somehow just didn't feel important anymore. I think one of the biggest things that bothers me to this day is… why? I will never know why, maybe he still doesn't either.

When I was forced to go back to school, I knew I had to find friendships somehow and chose ones that were more surface level because it was more comfortable at the time. I started drinking and smoking and eventually by the end of grade 12, I hadn't received all my credits required to graduate and was told I could not come back. I went from being someone who was good and pure to feeling like I didn't deserve good things in my life so I didn't allow myself to have them. What I did give myself though, was a voice. I became someone who was no longer shy and reserved and very outspoken. I made new friendships, some that were meaningful, others that were temporary, but I wasn't alone anymore.

My outlook on myself and relationships was that I was unworthy of love. I ended up finding a relationship that was meaningful to me only to sabotage it, because deep down I didn't love myself and I didn't believe I deserved it. I continued to have relationships that were unsuccessful because of the men I chose to have in my life. I wouldn't allow myself deep meaningful relationships because of a fear of being let down again, of being played. I chose relationships that I knew were toxic. If they seemed like they were actually going in a good place I would ruin it so that I felt like it was my choice, my decision.

I spent years of my life like this until I ended up in what was likely my most toxic relationship yet. But this relationship was also the best thing that ever happened to me because it gave me my daughter. Her biological dad left when I was twelve weeks pregnant and while it was heartbreaking at the time, I look back at it now and think this was the best thing that could have happened. Being a single mom from the start let me build up the strength I would need to raise my daughter right. While pregnant, I began to search deeper within for strength. My trauma might have caused me to not love myself but because of it, I wanted to push like hell to learn to love myself again before my daughter arrived on this planet.

This story almost started with the birth of my daughter. I feared that speaking of my darker parts might be too much. But then I remembered what held me back from loving myself was my ability to use my voice. Would my story be just that if I didn't include it? While my journey didn't begin with the birth of my daughter, I finally felt like I had a reason to live again. She gave me reason to love myself because she deserved a mother that would try. There were days then, and sometimes still now, where I felt myself falter.

But instead of letting it affect my self-worth, I allow myself grace and forgiveness and it's made a world of a difference.

Becoming a mom wasn't this magical fix for the way I viewed myself and my body though. It took a while to adjust to being a mom and the ways it changed my body. A big fear I had was that if I can't love and accept my body as it is now, how can someone else? My breasts were no longer as perky as they were pre-baby and pre-breastfeeding. My stomach wasn't as flat. There were stretch marks between my thighs, and a few on my stomach – and this all started affecting my self-perceived worth. I had tried so hard to not allow it to, though. It took time and hard work to get to where I am now and the journey of the first few years of motherhood was hard.

I ended up burning so many calories from being a single mom, breastfeeding and just doing it all solo, that I ended weighing much less than I did pre-pregnancy. I allowed that to give me more self-worth at the time and when I stopped breastfeeding and gained back weight I allowed that to impact how I felt about myself again. I would look back at pictures of myself from a few months earlier and compare the thickness of my thighs and hips. Memories would pop up on Facebook from back in my early '20s showing myself in my thinner body and much perkier breasts and I found these images to be extremely triggering, considering my relationship with food and exercise then was, what I realize now, extremely toxic.

A few years before pregnancy, like a lot of women

do, I spent some of my life obsessing over the scale, the amount of fat on my body, and comparing the way my body currently looked to how it looked prior. I was highly influenced by reading a book on "clean eating" and I let it take over my life. What I thought was a healthy decision for my body was actually the complete opposite. I would go away for weekends with friends to the cottage and would turn down all the amazing foods everyone else was eating and would spend time away from friends making my own meals. I would turn down invites to restaurants, fearful that there wouldn't be anything on the menu that was "clean" enough for me to eat.

I began going to the gym 5 – 6 times a week, running all the way there and pushing too hard on the weights all while consuming far too little calories for what I was burning off. Eventually, I ended up with a 50% tear in both of my rotator cuffs and tendinitis in both shoulders from pushing too fast and hard at the gym. I was told I needed to fully recover before I could continue, and fear took over. What if I gained all the weight back I had lost? What if I began to lose the definition I had worked so hard to get? If I wasn't all in, I couldn't do it—it was all or nothing[11] for me. Looking back now I can see this behaviour that I thought was healthy was not. I was just trying to fill a void.

---

11 And unfortunately, this "all or nothing" approach is *so* common among women trying to establish and maintain a healthy lifestyle. It doesn't have to be "all" versus "nothing". It can be integrative. It can be just doing the next best healthy thing for yourself, whether that's moving your body, making a healthy meal, drinking a big glass of water, journalling, meditating, or going to bed early. Remember that!

Accepting my postpartum body was different through. Unlike before, I didn't let it turn into an obsession because I had someone that would be looking up to me. The way I would speak about my body would become the language she would one day use to describe herself. And I wanted that to be with kindness and love. I think for me it took becoming a positive role model for someone else to really push me into loving myself more.

As I ventured further into motherhood, it's kind of comical when I think about it, but I stopped caring about wearing push up bras to "fix" my sagging breasts and I started wearing bras that were wire free. Somehow ditching the wire made me feel more accepting of the changes motherhood brought to my body. I started wearing high-waisted underwear that I felt comfortable in and somehow that made me feel empowered. I put aside the notion that I needed to dress and wear certain things because that's what society expected. I broke free from my limiting belief that I couldn't wear jeans because I didn't have a flat stomach and I started wearing what made me feel like me.

With this liberating feeling I began to surround myself with literature that spoke to me and gave me the tools it took to grow my love for myself. I found a community online filled with inspiration and uplifting accounts that spoke about self-love and accepting you for you. It pushed me into a renewed way of seeing myself. I started to view my body as something beautiful just as it was. And that feeling, I wanted to share that with not only my daughter but the world somehow.

Being someone who naturally thrives off helping others, I tend to put a lot of my worth in how I make others feel. Part of this is probably why I am able to have a successful business. But, I also have started to recognize that I cannot attribute my self-worth to others. Self-worth is something that comes from within; it's something that you give yourself not what you give to others. I see now that my self-worth is separate from what I can give to others but it is definitely something that has driven me to where I am now.

I ended up starting a boudoir photography business that focuses on self-love and acceptance. I wanted to showcase the beauty in each body, to help other women accept the things about themselves that society has brainwashed us into thinking are "flaws". Getting to meet women of all shapes and sizes, hearing about their own journey in self-love, and how they have learned to accept themselves for who they are, inspires my own journey and pushes me more into myself each day.

There's nothing quite like getting to see women transform in front of my eyes during a session. Doing something that is completely new to you can be scary as hell. Stepping outside of your comfort zone, booking a session – that's a big step. But walking into the studio, meeting someone for the first time, and feeling comfortable enough to bare it all during a session – now that's a leap. I get to witness the nervousness at the start of a session melt away as time goes on. It's like witnessing a transformation of oneself, and that is beautiful, there's just seriously nothing quite like it.

You might be wondering, what does someone else's transformation have to do with your own journey? This took me some time to truly understand as well. It goes back to my core values, those deep-set values that bring me happiness and purpose in my life. I took a lot of time to figure out what core values even were, let alone to figure out what mine were. But taking the time to figure this out and then build a business around it has added so much value to my life and has taken me further along my path than ever before.

Being allowed the space to uplift others by sharing images and stories of women, advocating for the acceptance of all bodies, it's an amazing feeling. But being able to share my own journey on this platform and being accepted for who I am, having other women relate to my stories and have it actually inspire them, it's a feeling like no other. For me, there is a certain feeling you get when something you say resonates with others, and it pushes me to keep being real, raw and vulnerable and that is what's encourage me to do the same here within my own chapter.

Because my own journey has a lot to do with inspiring others to embrace themselves, I want to do just that these last few paragraphs. I want you to finish this chapter know that you are not defined by your trauma. That the things you have been through, the things you have said or done because of the effects trauma has had on you, those things do not define you. You are worthy of love and growth and acceptance. These things are not always easy but what great things in life are?

Growing up being surrounded by brands promoting diet and detox pills, so that you can obtain that "perfect body", and a culture that fat shames, these program you into thinking that you hold your worth in your weight. Companies that push creams to rid you of your beautiful stretch marks or to banish your completely natural cellulite profit on your insecurities. They form an idea in our minds of this "ideal" and unattainable body, which makes you feel less about yours. It's confusing and makes your wonder if you even have the ability to be sexy in your own skin.

Do not allow them to control your worth. Better yet, do not allow anyone to control your worth. To the teenage girl settling for the boy who treats her wrong because she does not believe she is worthy of love: I see you. To the woman in her early 20s partying to fill the void left from those around her who made her feel anything less than beautiful: I see you. To the new mama who's struggling to accept the changes in her body while trying to push past the anxiety motherhood can cause: I see you.

You are beautiful.

You are worthy.

You are always enough.

So just be you!

KEY TAKEAWAY
Jennifer Green

@beyou.bou
@momfidentaf
#selfloveclub

CHAPTER SEVENTEEN

Kathleen Cameron

Kathleen is an Leader, Author, and Manifestation and Success Coach living in Ontario, Canada. With two Undergraduate Degrees and a Master's Degree, Kathleen started her leadership journey as a Registered Nurse. That journey expanded into entrepreneurship when she began in the Network Marketing industry in 2017. Kathleen quickly realized that working for herself and being present with her daughters was truly possible and went for it. Kathleen resigned from her senior leadership position in healthcare to be fully self-employed in 2019 and has never looked back! Now with three successful streams of income, including partnering with Bob Proctor, Kathleen helps others step into their true potential and become the best version of themselves with their goals met. Kathleen lives her life out loud sharing her journey of losing over 100 pounds, overcoming depression and illness, while #doingitforhergirls.

Find Kathleen:
@kathleencameron_formygirls | www.diamondacademy.ca

I started hating my body when I was seven years old. I remember not realizing I was any different until kids at school started calling me "fat" and a "pig". My parents had always told me I was beautiful and I believed it until someone told me otherwise[12]. I started wearing big baggy clothes and was that girl who wore a t-shirt into the swimming pool just to hide my body. I refused to do any sports, dance or swimming because I could not handle the jokes, the looks and the criticism. I became very aware of my body and how different it was from others, and inferior at that. I got my braces on when I was 10 years old. Just when I thought things couldn't get worse, they put giant metal brackets on my teeth. Overweight, frizzy hair and braces – just my luck! Kids are cruel and I was an easy target. The hardest part to admit was that at such a young age I hated myself and wished I was someone else.

I started starving myself when I was 11 years old. I remember hearing somewhere that if you drank a ton of water you would lose weight so I would throw my lunch in the garbage and drink nothing but water all day long. No matter how much I starved myself my body did not change and I could not figure out why! Was I meant to be this way forever?

---

12 Heartbreaking, and an unfortunate reality in so many of our stories. – Courtney

Would the jokes and comments ever stop? This continued until one day I realized this didn't work. So I gave up.

I started binge eating when I was 13 years old. I would come home from school relieved to be home but sad, very sad. Someone would have made fun of me at school and the only thing that made me feel better was food. I would eat whatever I could find until I felt sick. I would eat one portion in front of people and then come back for another when no one was looking. The food made me feel better. The sugar and the rush became my coping mechanism. I was just becoming a teenager and already developing bad habits that would continue on in my life. Being fat became my identity. I was the "fat" girl. Kathleen was lost.

I started smoking, drinking and doing drugs when I was 13 years old (sorry, Mom!). I honestly do not remember much about high school. Certain memories pop up, but not many. I think I blocked a lot of it out. A memory that pops up here and there was one day I went into my classroom, and I found a picture that my two best friends had drawn of me. In that drawing, they were making fun of how I was "as big as a house". I was destroyed. I became their friends again because what other choice did I have? No one liked me and I would rather be friends with them again then be alone. I smoked, drank and did drugs because I would at least fit in somehow. I can't tell you how many times I got told I had a "pretty face", that I needed to lose weight and to call Jenny Craig. I never felt pretty or feminine, wearing oversized clothes and always having my hair in a ponytail. I was embarrassed by how I looked most of the time. One of the worst memories was when someone told me I reminded them of Mimi from the Drew Carey Show. How horrifying. I yo-yo dieted for the next 10 years, always trying to measure up to that permanently idolized "body ideal". You know the one. I would lose weight then it would all come back. This is the story of my life, and I have since discovered that it is a similar story to so many others.

Because I was feeling like a failure in so many parts of my life, I began to excel at being a student. I spent seven years in University, completing two degrees and then a third when my first daughter was born. I could not control my body and how I treated it but I could be good at something, so I was determined to be successful in other areas of my life. I began working up the leadership ladder and found a skill in leading people. I had a caring and compassionate heart, so working with others became my niche. Being a nurse, and then a nurse leader, gave me pride because being overweight was never held over my head. I had a bigger purpose. Things got bad again not long after this.

I hit 306 pounds when I was 35 years old. I had my second daughter and was suffering from crippling postpartum depression. I was sad, unmotivated, and I ate all day. Being alone all day with two kids was miserable and I became hopeless. I started planning how I would end it all, feeling like everyone would be better off without me. I refused to get help until one day, after putting my plan in place and realizing just how far gone I was, I walked into a walk in clinic for help. The doctor at first would not treat me. He told me to see my family doctor, which I did not have.

Being a nurse myself, I told him I was not leaving until I got some help. I started on medication and within a couple weeks the cloud began to lift. That time of my life was the hardest. I have very few memories that make me smile and when I look back I have very few photos. Now that I am in a much better place I am saddened to think that I was so bad that I wanted to leave this earth. I could never imagine doing it now, so I know that my mind was not right and that reaching out for help was the best thing I ever did. Still to this day I go back to that darkness very quickly so I need to control my mind as much as possible.

After being off for 18 months, I went back to work. The job was awful. It was stressful and competitive and all I could do to cope with it all was to eat. Being somewhere for eight hours a day that you could not stand was hard, especially dreading it as soon as you would go to bed the night before. I was either at work or dreading being there. At my heaviest weight, I was struggling the most, not as much emotionally but physically. My body hurt everywhere, my knees, my hips, and my back. My bladder wouldn't hold through the night and going up a flight of stairs was exhausting. I knew everyone around me was worried, I could see it in their eyes but knew they felt like they couldn't say anything without hurting my feelings. My blood pressure was high, I had a fatty liver and my brother had just had his third or fourth heart attack. My future was looking pretty bleak. Something had to give.

I was 35 when I decided to take my life back. I had met someone through social media. She was successful, we had a lot in common, and she offered me hope. We talked a lot about her business, her community and she believed in me. She saw something in me that I didn't. With her help, I decided to start my health journey and start a business that I could do completely via social media. I went LIVE for the first time proclaiming to the social media world (and the two live viewers) that I was losing the weight! The next year was life changing. I dropped 100 pounds, made hundreds of new friends and renewed old connections and grew a successful social marketing business. The support I received kept me going and human connection brought me out from under hating myself.

I focused so much on my mindset that I convinced myself that I was worthy and that I could get healthy and build a business. I immersed myself in reading personal development books, listening to podcasts, delving into this inspiring community of woman and visualizing myself happy and healthy. It worked. It took discipline. What I mean by that is discipline to focus on my mindset, focus on the future I was creating and to follow the commands I gave myself. How many times have you told yourself you will eat healthy tomorrow and then binge all day? I did this all the time. The more I did this the more I lost the belief in myself that I would ever be able to commit and actually follow through. By working on my thoughts I was able to raise that self-belief, then start following my own commands which grew my faith and hope of a brighter future. By reading this book you are filling your mind with stories of hope and this will help you for sure!

I ran my first 10 kilometre race at 35 years old. I had been training for months. I was shocked with how much I was able to do since I started training only a few months before. I could barely run a full minute, never mind 10 kilometres without stopping! I finished the race in one hour and 30 minutes, my fastest time ever. The race was a sign for me. It showed me that I could do anything I set my mind to. I had done something I never thought I could! I gave myself commands over and over again and followed them. Things had changed – I was different.

I was 36 years old when my 6-year-old daughter came home and told me she was being called fat at school and at dance class. I thought going through this myself growing up was hard, this felt much worse. All the emotion came back but this time with anger. How can kids be so cruel? A 6-year-old child who is beautiful, innocent and so impressionable. It breaks my heart. When I tell people that, their first comment is to put her on a "diet". Hold up – what? I do not want to teach my daughters they need to lose weight to be liked or for the bullying to stop. I want them to know they are beautiful right now, no matter what their external body looks like. What we look like does not define us. It is merely a picture of who we are. We are on the inside, we are a spirit in a body, a body that is here to allow us to live on this earth. Our focus should be on health, not outward appearance. I am determined to make sure my daughters will never hate themselves like I did. I will tell them they are beautiful every single day. I will not leave this alone. This is when I started questioning the idea that was planted in my head all my life that I was not as worthy because I was overweight.

I started loving myself at 36 years old. Not after I lost all the weight, but once I started gaining some of it back. My body was happy with me, I could feel it. My pain was gone, bladder issues resolved, no more heartburn. The fat on my liver had reduced significantly and my blood pressure significantly lower. So many amazing changes in my body, but as you know, things do not always stay positive forever. I had lost 102 pounds and was the healthiest I had ever been but started going unconscious 3-4 times per week continuously for months and months. No one knew what was wrong. I dropped in Walmart, Costco, in the car, at work. It was humiliating. I was in and out of the ER, had a hospital admission and too many doctor's appointments and tests to list here. One of the hardest days was when I lost my drivers' license.

Losing my independence was hard. I had already stopped driving so this was only a formality but it made things much more serious. With no diagnosis yet in sight, I was sad and afraid. I could tell people around me were worried and that I was scaring my young daughters. I continued to work full time, worried every second that I was going to drop in a meeting with executives or that I would faint in my office and hurt myself while alone. I kept all these concerns to myself and pressed on. My husband took a lot of the slack. He would spend more than three hours a day in the car driving the girls to school, me to work, then himself to work. I would be on the couch most evenings too tired to do anything. Everyone was telling me to stop working, even my doctor, but for some reason I felt like I would be letting people down. When I realized I was letting my own family down, I decided to take some time off work that the doctors recommended.

It became so normal for me to just randomly faint that others who weren't witness to it as often thought we were all nuts for acting so calm. I had one test that proved the diagnosis and course of treatment. It was a tilt table test. It was awful and scary. They caused me to faint so they could monitor me. My blood pressure and heart rate were dropping so low when relaxed that I couldn't remain conscious. They diagnosed me with Vaso-Vagal Syncope. I started on cardiac meds and the fainting started to decrease over time. I had worked so hard to lower my blood pressure and here these meds were bringing it back up. I had also started eating again to feed my emotions. Weight started coming back on, and fast. I was starting to feel ugly again. Then someone else came into my life at that moment for a reason.

I met this amazing woman when I was gaining some of my weight loss back. She was so confident in herself and advocated for body positivity. She had gained some weight and started experiencing what society offers plus size woman and she was having none of it. She invited me to come pose in lingerie or underwear in Toronto and stand for all bodies being beautiful. My first response was: "no way!" I knew then that this was when I needed to change how I loved myself. Even after losing all this weight, I still couldn't show my bare belly off.

I was 36 years old when I posed in my bra and underwear for the first time in public. On April 27th I stood at the base of the CN TOWER with 12 other people in a body positivity movement. I posed for photos in a lacy bra and underwear showing my stomach for the first time ever with pride. I posed to advocate for and change the social stigma associated with being overweight. I am making it my mission to change the paradigm and inspire people to love themselves more. I was made to feel unworthy my entire life for being overweight and I believed it until now. I posed for my second photo shoot in Niagara Falls a few months later and took my daughters with me. I wanted to show them a group of woman proud of their bodies, confident and posing for pictures, and I was one of them! I realized that I had lost all the weight for the wrong reasons. I did it initially to be skinny, to fit in, and to meet the societal ideal of a beautiful body. I didn't even love myself at my smallest, but I sure do now!

I was 36 years old when someone used the word inspiring to describe me. It's not easy to talk about my successes. It almost feels like bragging, but if I am true to myself and my bigger purpose to help others find their path to self-love then I know I need to speak of them. Once I started to love myself and truly believe I was capable of far more than I ever thought was is when successes continued to come. My social marketing business continued to grow. I was able to inspire others to start their own health journey and love themselves more. So many people getting healthy and looking and feeling their best right before my eyes. So many woman chose to start successful businesses and I got to be a part of helping them step outside of their comfort zone and become their best!

As time went on, more and more people reached out to me about their journeys and how much they hated their bodies and in turn themselves. I listened to what the universe was telling me and chose to learn more about the mind and become a coach. I now get the incredible honour to help others transform their lives and create mindset shifts and in turn success. I am so passionate about self-image and get incredible joy in helping others create a positive self-image and become the person that has been hidden behind so many societal expectations for far too long.

I have released the desire to be someone I am not. I have released other people's opinions of me and any classification anyone placed on me. I now release weight for the right reasons; health, longevity, body movement and strength. I choose who I am and have chosen to be someone who lifts others up, who inspires and who is a good example. I know that by stepping into myself and becoming the best version of me is what allows me to help people on a bigger scale. Nothing brings me more happiness than seeing another woman realize what she is capable of, and watch her go after her dreams. I am no longer the person I thought I was for so many years. I have released her and stepped into my true self. I am inspirational. I am strong. I am driven. I am successful. I am me. I am proud.

You might feel like self-love is not possible for you, but one thing I want you to know is that you have the control of how you feel about yourself. No one else has that control. We often give the power to others when the power lies within. When you stop living on the outside and start living on the inside, you take back the power taken from you so long ago. There were several things I gave up along the way and I would highly suggest you give them up now too.

I have released caring about other people's opinions, whether real or not. I no longer speak negatively to myself or talk down to myself. If I find myself heading in that direction I immediately tell myself five things I love about myself. You cannot think both positively and negatively at the same time so it flips the switch right away. Another thing I gave up is comparing myself to others. When you focus on what others are doing you are not focusing on yourself. When someone is "in the zone", they have no clue what others are doing, neither do I. The hardest but most impactful thing I stopped doing was looking in the mirror in disgust and thinking something negative about my physical appearance. Now I look in the mirror and find something beautiful, or something I think looks nice.

While I released certain things from my life, I also added some pretty powerful strategies. I have a morning routine that starts my day strong. I raise my energy so that I feel unstoppable. I do gratitude, visualization, affirmations and mirror work. As I said before, I look at myself in the mirror and compliment myself. I also keep track of things that make me feel good and go to them when I feel low. I often give myself reminders of what I am capable of since I no longer need external validation, I get that within. I do many of these things again before bed as well.

For 28 years, I thought I was fat, ugly and unwanted. It wasn't until I started sharing my story that I realized I was not alone. I have since learned that through sharing our stories we come together and support each other so for that reason I share mine here. My goal for the rest of my time on this earth is to empower others with my message with the hopes of helping others to love themselves. The moment you fall in love with yourself your whole world changes. I have two successful businesses, a beautiful family and a vision for my future so big that it scares peoples around me. I know what I am capable of and I am going for it. Self-love is not just recommended, it's necessary.

KEY TAKEAWAY
Kathleen Cameron

@kathleencameron_formygirls
@momfidentaf
#selfloveclub

CHAPTER EIGHTEEN

Lisa Simmons

Lisa Simmons is the CEO and mastermind behind *Lisa K Simmons*. She resides in London, Ontario with her family where she builds a life of love and passion. Through navigating life as an Oncology Nurse, Mother and a new diagnosis of Anxiety and Depression, Lisa found her strengths.

Lisa is a business coach, the creator of *The Body Series* and the proud designer of a line of Empowerment T-Shirts. Lisa is here to empower, to light the fire and ignite bravery within those who desire to change their story. Lisa truly believes that together, we can do anything.

Find Lisa:
@itslisaksimmons | www.lisaksimmons.com

Life has a lot to offer this day and age. A lot of feels, a lot of confusion, and a lot of information. These days, it's easier to know what the term self-love means, but a decade ago? A decade ago, I didn't recognize the value or the impact loving myself would truly have on the person I am today. It's one thing to know what self-love means and it's another thing to put the term to work. Today, I know. And, man, oh, man, do I wish I knew this before. Let me preface this by saying, I don't have all the secrets. I've gone through life the same as you: succeeding, failing, and learning as I go. That's what I'm going to share with you. What I've gone through and how it has helped.

So, here we are. We start life on this planet with a fresh canvas. We are empty, yet filled with love. We grow and we learn and eventually all our innocence slowly disappears. I don't exactly know when it happens—you know, the moment our innocent minds turn into ones filled with everything else. Filling us with pain, judgement, fear, and worry. I may not know the age my life changed, but I do have my memories. I know that while preparing for my tenth grade picture day, for some reason I thought I needed a tighter shirt—one that showed off my chest. I know that on summer break I wanted to wear a bikini and was subsequently asked, "Are you sure you want to wear that?" I remember being paranoid at school dances that a slow song would come on and no one would ask me to dance. I know the feeling I had when I got dumped by my first love and felt so much resentment toward my body. The list is long.

These memories don't define me; they are simply chapters in my story. Though I had many lessons throughout my childhood, the most powerful ones came as an adult in the last twelve years. Let's fast forward to adulthood.

In 2009, I was 23. I graduated from McMaster University with my Nursing Degree and was working a full-time job on an inpatient Oncology ward in Ottawa. It was the first time in my life I needed to always put other people first. Those people were my patients. My top priority every day was to give them the best care possible, to solve as many problems as I could, and to leave knowing I'd gone above and beyond. I came home depleted, but the tricky part was I felt a sense of reward at the end of each day. I knew I did a great job and that my patients were in good hands so I kept going back. I did this for days, months, even years. For all those years, I had blinders on. I still felt a nagging emptiness, despite my sense of accomplishment. This was because I was blind to my own needs, things as simple as eating regular meals. It soon escalated to not seeing my friends or going to social events. I went to work, came home, and that was it. On my days off, I could barely function. I became extremely emotional, feeling angry, sad, and empty, both at work and at home. Before I knew it, I was lost and broken. As more time passed, the person who got lost was completely out of sight. I had become a stranger to myself. I didn't see it coming and maybe I should have. Luckily, I have people in my life who gave me a reality check and from then on, I knew I needed to make changes.

I needed to start somewhere. I needed to find the parts of life I hadn't seen in a long time. The parts that lit me up and made me feel alive. I also needed to find meaning, JOY, and most importantly, stabilize my mental health. So, I started reading. I made it a habit to read as much as I could. The time I spent with my head in books was the quality time I needed to help me recharge and find out how I got to where I was right now: miserable and exhausted.

What did I really need? I needed self-love. Reading gave me that. It allowed me to sit with myself, to break down what was happening and really let myself sit with being uncomfortable. (Okay, you may be thinking, "uncomfortable"?! WTF, you're reading a book, how is that "uncomfortable"? What I mean is, it's not easy to sit still and do something for yourself when you're used to giving all of yourself to other people. It's not easy to read pages in a book that feel like personal attacks on your life. It may be easy to read lines in a book, but it's not always easy to piece it all together. Reading was the first stepping stone but I needed more.)

What was next? I took up running. I slowly grew to love what is known as the "runner's high." Not only did I feel on top of the world after a good 5K, the feeling during the run was what got me hooked. I was able to do a lot of reflecting on the trails along the canal of the Ottawa River. I ran so I could empty my head and, for a long time, it was great. I distracted myself by working towards new goals—5K, 10K and Half Marathons. Running had become my great escape. Running was ultimately my saving grace because through running I found something else. As some people may know, running isn't gentle on the body. It can be hard and gruelling at times, and for me, resulted in injury after injury.

In an attempt to heal some injuries and stretch my muscles, I took up yoga. I went with a friend who suggested I give it a try. My first class was strange and unfamiliar. I remember some giggles, some "what the f*&$" moments, and some ah-ha ones, too. Even though I didn't love what was happening while I was in yoga class, I decided to keep going. I remember the exact class that changed it all for me: I remember the location I set-up my mat, I remember the decor inside the studio, the warm temperature and the people around me. That day, I came to class and unrolled my mat. It started out like any other yoga class would. I listened, went along with the movements and allowed myself to be guided. At the end of class, we were in savasana, which is the final resting pose of the class, and is usually coupled with a closing meditation. The teacher began to bring us through a short guided meditation with the visualization of an orb of light. The orb of light represented our ego and our love for ourselves. I lay and allowed myself to become completely entranced by the light. I envisioned the light, the beautiful golden orb swirling above my heart space. I felt weightless. I woke up from the meditation with tears streaming down my face. It was a powerful moment for me. In that moment, I knew I had found the first real steps toward healing what was broken within me.

I continued to run, but became a regular at the yoga studio. I started to feel subtle shifts within myself. I no longer felt guilty putting time aside for me. I began to realize, I loved my life outside of work again, and in turn, was starting to love myself and the person I was becoming. I had more patience, I was less harsh on myself and people around me, and slowly, my happiness was beginning to grow.

The yoga studio I attended started transitioning to new owners and at that time, I began practicing at another studio with the same friend that brought me to my first class. I met a teacher there who was unlike any of the others I had ever met. Authentic, real, and genuine. Classes can be uniform in the way they are structured, which involves giving guidance through typical popular asanas, sun-salutations, and other postures; just the regular, run-of-the-mill class. The teacher I found within this new studio wasn't like that. When she taught, you could tell it was from a different place. Not an "I just love yoga" type of teaching, it was a "this will change your fucking life if you want it to" type of teaching. Her name was Erin.

The intent was always strong and somehow always relatable for me. My breath was different. My movements were different. My state of mind was different. My openness, my emotions, everything was different. I became a regular in her classes and I made it a priority to get myself there. I needed what she offered. Through the clarity I received through these small acts of self-love, I knew my work life needed to change. I continued to work at the hospital but I transitioned to being part-time. I knew I needed to separate myself from what was depleting me of my energy.

Then, something crazy happened. I was working a night shift and found myself sitting with a friend while we were on break, talking about yoga. I told her I had an interest in teaching, so we started to look at trainings in the city. We did some Google searches and we found out Enlightenment Yoga was offering a Yoga Teacher Training (YTT) in a couple months. Coincidentally, the teacher training program happened to be instructed by the same teacher I had been going to classes with for months now.

I signed up the next day. The 200-hour intensive training would take place over a 30-day period. The program would be every day and I would need to take time off work. I didn't know how I could get the time off but to me, that didn't matter. I made it happen and in July 2014, I started. Back then I thought I wanted to become a yoga teacher and though that's the story I told myself, it wasn't true. The reason I took this training was to heal and transform.

There are times in all of our lives that we create stories about decisions we make in order to put a Band-Aid on our feelings. We cover up our feelings so we don't have to acknowledge them. These Band-Aids hide pain. A couple examples of Band-Aids from my personal experience can be anything from shopping to food to abusing substances. Band-Aids may cover the problem, but they don't make it go away. There is a time and a place for Band-Aids, don't get me wrong. There will always be an instance where all you need is a Band-Aid, something to distract you and then you can move on. In some instances, though, there will be situations where the problem runs much deeper and it's too late for a simple cover-up. Running was a Band-Aid for me but it was a time in my life when I needed more.

When I sought out the training, I undervalued myself. Though I was starting to feel freer again, I wanted more (again). Little did I know this training would be the start of a long and healing journey. I completed my intensive training in August 2014. During the 30 days, I cried, I laughed, and I grew more than I could have ever imagined. There were days I wanted to go and there were also days where I would curse, swear and literally drag myself out of bed to get there. A lot happened over that month of July. We did "sharing circles," (...and I know you're now probably thinking the experience was filled with that kind of 'woo woo' shit. I hear you. I thought the same thing at first, honestly. But now I realize that type of experience is truly the most transformative form of therapy.) We did meditations, visualizations, and a daily ninety-minute Yoga practice. Though I was trained in Hatha Yoga, our daily practices were in Forest Yoga. Forest Yoga is the type of practice Erin teaches in all her public classes, like the ones I was taking at the studio. The breath work is targeted, the movements are held for long periods, and sequenced in a way that invites healing to the body. Our bodies hold emotions and trauma and for those who believe, it really can change your life.

I went from sitting slumped over to hide from myself to being proud to sit up straight.

I went from being a victim to being brave.

I went from hiding my voice to knowing my worth.

After completing the training, I returned back to work a different person. I was now part-time but demanded to be removed from working night shifts or I was going to quit. *NOTE: I don't recommend doing this. It was right for me but is NOT everyone's cup of tea.* A few months later, I left the ward. It was too draining for me and knowing my body and mind needed more rest, I went into the outpatient clinics. And life became different for me.

When you align with yourself, when you truly give yourself the time to decompress, when you remove the guilt and know your worth, you see clearly. The blinders go away. You know what's best for you, because you've given yourself the gift of you.

You may have noticed that through these stories I've mentioned work and friends but never a partner. For years, I dated, and for years, I got dealt some pretty crappy people. By the time I was 29, I was ready for what I deserved. I began to look back and review what I'd learned over the years, and one of the methods that rang true across all my reading and through my Yoga Training was the power of manifestation. Since I lived alone, I took out some chalk and wrote all over my walls. I may sound crazy right now, but that's exactly what I did. I wrote down all the positive things I had in my life and all the characteristics I wanted in a partner.

Here are a few of the words I wrote across my walls:

LOYAL.

HEALTHY.

HANDSOME.

SELF-SUFFICIENT.

CONFIDENT.

KIND.

FUN.

LOVING.

I would walk by these words multiple times a day. I saw them, I lived them, and eventually, I found them. I never would have gotten there if I didn't put in the work. I spent years dating and years learning lessons because I didn't truly know myself enough to love *me*. Now, I had done the work. I put in the time with myself and I was ready.

Who knew that one tinder swipe, an exchange of a number and one date later would make the rest history. It almost seemed too simple. With Ricardo, it was easy, our relationship happened at warp speed. "I love you's" at 3 months, moving in together at 6 months, engaged at 9 months and a move across the pond at 12 months. It was picture perfect. We both kept active social lives, some separate and some together. I totally had this down-pat. I could have it all – loving myself and someone else too.

My love story sounds pretty incredible, right? Right. So, let's talk about England for a hot minute. Keep in mind that throughout my whole adult life, I have been completely self-sufficient. Supporting myself financially, travelling, living alone and for most of my life, I was single. In June 2016, I quit my job, we packed our bags, and we moved to Oxford, England.

You guys, England ruined me. It striped me of my autonomy, my anchors and freakin' SUNSHINE. I felt like I got catapulted back through all my years of transformation. I was miserable again, but this time, I wasn't working. The hospital couldn't be to blame. I didn't understand what was happening to me. I hated leaving the house, but I also sort of hated being there, too. I was paranoid with every new place we went. I started having insomnia which was worse in unfamiliar places. I forgot what a good night's sleep felt like.

In the summer of 2016, Ricardo and I went to Greece. It was incredible, minus the fact that I was nauseous 50% of the time and not sleeping the other 50% of the time. I would lay awake crying, my body and brain were so tired but would not allow me to sleep.

I understand why now, but for years, I didn't.

Months passed and we didn't know where the next year would take us. Ricardo was on a year contract with his fellowship but he was considering doing a PhD in London, which would land us in England for another 3-5 years. England was already HARD. His family lives in Brazil, mine in Canada, and we had ZERO friends. To say the least, it was a bit defeating. Could I survive another 5 years?

You're probably asking yourself what happened. How did I spiral from being so happy to struggling? What happened was, the Band-Aids I had been using were no longer enough. There was no yoga practice to heal my wounds; there were no distractions to save me. Sometimes along our journey, self-love isn't enough. Self-love is vital to having a healthy mind but sometimes life throws us a speed bump that we can't control. And that bump can take us out of the driver's seat.

In February 2017, we got news we never expected. We were pregnant. I'll never forget the night we went and got the pregnancy test. I felt sick the whole drive in the car, not because of morning sickness, but because I was so nervous. I remember being alone in the bathroom, you know, peeing on the stick. I looked down and immediately saw the test was positive. I cried. Ricardo came in thinking I was crying happy tears and for about a month, I let him believe that's what they were - happy. They were not happy tears, you guys. I wanted to travel, to enjoy my time with Ricardo, to make friends, to feel free. But, like they say, there is never a perfect time for a baby.

It never crossed our mind to end the pregnancy. We knew we wanted to keep the baby. We made the decision to move back to Canada and Ricardo would look for work there. When I finished my first trimester, I moved back to Canada alone and Ricardo joined me two months later when his fellowship was over in Oxford. For months, I struggled. I was back into a cycle of not putting myself first. I put the baby first and then Ricardo. They needed me and what I didn't realize was who needed me the most was actually me. I did need me but I needed more too.

Ricardo landed in Canada in April and by mid-summer he had a job, ironically enough, in London, but this time London, Ontario. In August 2017, we moved into a two-bedroom apartment and started our life in a new city.

On October 20th, 2017 at 11:38am, Noah was born at the Victoria Hospital. What a ride that was. I'll spare you all the details but let's just say, I was unmedicated and it was quick. Noah rushed into the world as fast as he surprised us back in February. The months that passed were scary. Motherhood, guys. Ouuuffff. That shit should come with a manual.

Now, don't get me wrong. I love Noah with my entire being; he was brought to me in this life to make me who I am today. My transition to being a mom was not easy. Ricardo still tells people to this day, that he was caring for two children when I was postpartum. If it isn't obvious, I was one of the children. I went to see a counsellor a couple times. No one thought I had post-partum depression or the baby blues and they weren't wrong. I had good days and bad days. Good days were mediocre and the bad days usually happened at night. As you know, I've experienced insomnia before, but this time when it came I felt out of control. I would toss and turn, and kick and scream. I would move from bed to couch, pacing back and forth, and before I knew it Noah would be awake. This would continue until the sun came up. In the morning, I'd rebound. Normal morning, cool and collected, I'd nap when Noah napped, etc. But this cycle - it made me feel crazy. I felt like I was two different people: Lisa during the day and the Big Bad Wolf at night.

This went on for six months until we were in Brazil visiting Ricardo's family. Ricardo had to go vote so we were driving to a local polling station and out of nowhere, I told him I needed to tell him something. I started to cry which wasn't unusual but somehow this time it was different. I cried and the words could barely come. Through broken speech, I told Ricardo I had thoughts of ending my life. It was the hardest thing I've ever had to share because I knew it was true but at the same time, I felt the thoughts were not mine. The best way I can describe it is that when they came on, they felt like an out-of-body experience. They would come and go with no warning signs.

Ricardo was pretty shaken, rightfully so. The next day I went to see a psychiatrist. Now keep in mind, we are still in Brazil, so Ricardo had to find someone who could speak English since their first language there is Portuguese. I don't remember how long we talked but it felt like forever. I remember the feeling I had when the doctor told me I had depression and severe anxiety. I didn't feel bad, I felt relief.

The next day, on my 32nd birthday, I started anti-depressants. You read that right—my birthday. For some, it may seem crazy to start on such a special day but to me, it was the perfect time to start fresh. Within a week or so, I felt a bit different but the real change didn't come until months later when I found myself in the car with Ricardo again. Again, I was crying, this time though, I wasn't upset. This time it was because we were driving by a park, the trees were full of colour, the grass was green, the sky, a stunning hue of blue. It was beautiful. I had been waiting for this moment, the moment when things were beautiful again. Months prior, I asked the psychiatrist how I would know I was feeling better and he said, "You'll know. Things will look different."

Looking back now, I can see a pattern. Every time my life presented me with something new, I left myself behind.

Start of my career: "Bye Lisa!"

Big move overseas: "See ya later, L!"

Arrival of Noah: "Sayonara!"

Are there patterns in your life too? Do you forget about yourself when life gets tough? Life *will* test you. You're going to think you've got life figured out and then the universe throws you a curve ball to ask you, 'are you sure you've got this?' The world wants to know you're really in it and you're going to give it your all. I know my story is unlike most. It doesn't have a happy plot, it has one of growth and strength. My biggest takeaway is to listen to yourself. Your feelings when you need love and when you need help too may not feel the same; my best advice is to recognize them. Embody the feelings, let yourself move through them, journal, and if you feel drawn to, speak to someone you trust.

Today, I walk through life with a different mindset. I am gentle to myself. I give myself days of rest, I allow my life to flow at a speed that's comfortable. I made it through depression on medication, but that's not the end of my story. Medication treats my chemical imbalance, but what helped me shift my life faster than waiting for my desired outcome, was taking time for me and putting myself first. I allowed self-love into my life with a never-ending invitation. It is here to stay. I journal, I attend sound-baths, I meditate, I move my body, I hire coaches, and all of this personal work functions as tools to help me move through my past so instead of dwelling on it, I use my past as lessons for my present and future life. The effort we put into ourselves is a direct reflection of who we are.

Not everyone's journey to self-love is linear, in fact, likely no one's is. Know that along your path to happiness and radical self-love, there will be hurdles. The hurdles are just that though, hurdles to climb over, and you *can* climb over them. Your path doesn't have to be filled with pain, lessons and heartache either. It can be simple. It can start early. It can start with presence and awareness. Every day you can *choose* to walk past a mirror and see something beautiful: the colour of your skin, your eyes, your hair, the fabric of your shirt. As time passes, it will become second nature. One day the beauty will stare you back in the face. Why? Because you've been there the whole time. Sometimes, it just takes practice to find it.

KEY TAKEAWAY

Lisa Simmons

@itslisaksimmons
@momfidentaf
#selfloveclub

CHAPTER NINETEEN

Kerstin Foster & Jerrica Irwin

Kerstin Foster

Kerstin Foster is a Sales Account Manager, Entrepreneur and proud mother of two who has always had an undercover love for writing. Since having kids, Kerstin felt a shift in how she experienced her own self image and is passionate about sharing her journey to help other women on their own path to self love and acceptance.

With a background in investigations in the banking industry and her current full time career in sales, Kerstin's foray into the clothing design industry was definitely surprising. In 2017, while shopping with her sister Jerrica for a simple black t-shirt for her six month old son, they realized it was near impossible to find exactly what they were after. In that moment, they decided to start their own business and begin designing children's clothing with their brand Little Canuck. A year later, they designed a pair of pants for adults that were a huge hit, and their second brand Everday Hustle was born.

Kerstin is passionate about ethical clothing and human rights in the fashion industry, and the choices that are made for Everyday Hustle reflect these values. Kerstin resides just outside of Toronto with her husband Desric, fur baby Fenelon and two children, Hendrix and Harlow.

Jerrica Irwin

Jerrica is a Sales Representative by day and entrepreneur by night. As co-founder and owner of the clothing brand *Everyday Hustle*, she has a passion for spreading the word about ethical clothing manufacturing and sustainable fashion.

In 2017, Jerrica first co-founded *Little Canuck* with her sister Kerstin, a children's clothing brand ethically made in Canada. After getting a great response and receiving feedback that adults also loved the pieces, they launched their second brand, *Everyday Hustle*, in 2018.

Jerrica brings a diverse background to the brand and loves the creative outlet of designing new pieces. Working with her sister and best friend has been a dream come true, and being able to build and grow two ethically responsible Canadian brands is the cherry on top

Jerrica is a fur-mama to her dog Gus and a proud Auntie to her niece and nephew, Harlow and Hendrix.

@everyday.hustle | www.shopeverydayhustle.com
Author Photos: Autumn Leaf Photography

In today's society, self-love can feel a little bit…weird. With almost the entire world on social media judging what everyone else is doing and telling you what you need to do in order to love yourself, it's becoming more and more important to know who you are and know what is best for you. Following along other people's journeys for inspiration is great, but sometimes seeing so much self-love and body positivity discussion flooding your feed can have the opposite affect and make you start to question yourself. When everyone else is all about their own self-love and you aren't, is there something wrong? Do I force myself and pretend in order to "fit in" to this social media movement? Are all these people really friends or are they just Instagram friends? Is it okay to exercise and lose weight if that makes you feel better, or does that mean you don't love yourself the way you already are? We are here to tell you that it is OKAY to not be quite there yet. It's okay to have days where you feel not all 'In your feelings' about you, because we have those days too. We *all* do. Trust.

When we sat down to write this chapter, we both had imposter feelings – who the hell are we to be writing on this topic? We aren't experts! Do we even love ourselves enough to be suggesting to other people how to love themselves? The thing is, we AREN'T experts, we are just regular women and we think that's why it's important to share our story. It's important to be included in this book among all these amazing women, because we are amazing women too[13]. We feel that the self-love journey is a never ending one and that everyone is somewhere different along their own path.

As sisters, we grew up in the same house, with the same values and the same loving parents. We are lucky to have parents who have always accepted us for who we are and always made us feel comfortable. They always encouraged us to do what makes us happy and never pushed us to do things we didn't want to do. We have such close relationships with both of our parents as well as our extended family which provides such a great foundation for our own self-love. This chapter will take you through our individual stories and some significant moments in our lives that have had impact on our self-love journeys.

KERSTIN

Part of what I feel has made me love myself is being able to reflect on my past experiences and really analyze why I am the way I am. Acceptance of myself, acceptance of my past and to tie that together, acceptance of myself *despite* my past. Like most people, I have had waves throughout my life that have slipped me into lows and lifted me back up to be on top of the world. It's taken a long time, but what I can say that I really do commend myself for is my resilience. The comeback is always stronger than the set-

---

13 COULD 👏 NOT 👏 AGREE 👏 MORE — Courtney St Croix

back, isn't that what they say?

I was a competitive dancer for as long as I can remember and I loved it so much. My whole heart went into my practice and I loved everything about it. I always felt confident and I loved being on stage. The rush of putting it all out there and pushing myself to my very max kept me going year after year. I felt myself comparing my body and ability to other dancers as a regular day-to-day thing, but it never felt negative to me. I never had negative thoughts about my body or ability because of it; for me it was always motivation to see a friend or competitor that was better at something than I was. We weren't handed our awards and scholarships, we worked our asses off for them, and it felt damn good to achieve them. Understanding at such a young age that my skill was in my own hands to improve and keep building was my first empowering moment. The beautiful art I could create with my body just by focusing and working hard was such an amazing feeling. It made me proud to be *me* and proud of my abilities.

When I was in grade five, I ran into the first major experience that shook my self-confidence. I was bullied by a girl who (only as an adult, I now understand), was jealous of the security I had in myself and the friendships I had made. She was mean spirited and I was not. She would say nasty things about me to everyone and eventually had most of my friends pulled into her circle and I was suddenly alone at recess. I started asking the teacher if I could help in the classroom at recess instead of having to go outside and be alone. It was rough, it made me hate going to school. It made me anxious thinking about classic school requests, like 'picking a partner' or getting 'into groups'. It was terrible. I didn't understand what was so wrong with me and why she hated me so much. After quite a while, I told my parents and my mom called the school on multiple occasions but nothing was really done. My parents told me that I needed to stick up for myself and that if anything happened, they would have my back. It ended up coming to the point where this bully pushed me at recess in front of everyone and I just felt this overwhelming feeling to fight back. Knowing that I was supported by my parents after having no one else's support throughout the situation gave me the confidence to fight for myself. I shoved her with the kind of strength I didn't even know I had inside me. Now, please know that I *do not* promote violence in any way. But… after that she never bothered me again. I think that single act of confidence was all that was needed to break her down. I felt on top of the world, not because I had physically hurt someone, but because it was like I almost instantly got my life back. My friends started to include me in things again, there was no one saying mean things about me and I wasn't nervous to go to school every morning. I was proud that despite her breaking me down daily, I knew deep down that I was worth more than how I was being treated.

Then came high school, and subsequently, "the boy"… I think you probably know the one I mean. The one you have the biggest crush on, the one you would be so lucky to be with – yeah, that one. When he finally asked me out,

I felt like I had won the high school cheerleader's lottery! Everything was great at first. We were cute, went to all the parties with his friends that were outside my circle of friends. I wore his jacket in the halls; he waited at my locker. You know, typical Zack and Kelly from *Saved By the Bell* stuff. That's the funny thing about this kind of relationship, it's a gradual fall downhill so you aren't so quick to catch yourself. He was so kind and caring and complimentary at the beginning. It started with the two of us hanging out more than I hung out with my own friends. A little longer into the relationship there were small comments about other girls being 'so pretty' and asking me why I didn't do my makeup like 'that girl' when we were walking in the mall. It eventually led to him pinching my stomach when I was sitting on the couch, 'joking' that it looked like I had gained some weight since I had been on break from dance. Writing this is actually quite cringe worthy for me and pretty embarrassing as I know friends and family will read this that don't really know the whole story, but I feel like it is important to include and that it's a large part of the person I have become today. His comments and criticism didn't make me upset with him, it made me upset with myself. Anyone who knows me today would never imagine I would put up with someone treating me that way, but it's difficult to understand a master manipulator unless you have lived it AND come out on the other side of it.

I used to jog to his house in the mornings on summer break so that I could burn extra calories, since I wasn't dancing in the summer. If you know me and are reading this, you may not even believe that since you know how much I am NOT a morning person. When I got to his house, I would do a pretty strenuous workout with him to 'support' his training (he was on a couple sports teams and trained nearly every day) and then most of the time would go to the gym later in the evening if we weren't hanging out or I wasn't working at my part time job, all the while making sure I was eating restricted calories. By no means am I saying that being so active isn't great under regular circumstances, but I was really doing it to make sure I could avoid his comments if I stayed in the best shape. What I didn't realize at the time is that it didn't matter what I did, his comments were really a reflection of his own issues and how much he disliked himself. I was miserable and I thought it was all my fault. My friends would tell me that he treated me like crap and I would defend him. I always had an excuse about why he was a shitty person and I was always trying to fix it, so much so that I lost myself in the process. I became so wrapped up in maintaining this relationship that I forgot who I was as a person. After all, if he was with me so much and thought these things about me, then it had to be true, right? This went on for quite some time; we were together for over two years.

After multiple break ups and make ups, I was walking out of school one day and a girl asked if she could talk to me. She pulled me aside from my group of girlfriends and nervously told me that she had been hanging out with my boyfriend. MY boyfriend. She had a voicemail from him on her phone, and she let me listen to it. I was enraged and embarrassed, not with her but with myself and with the person I had defended all this time. This wasn't the first time I had been given questionable news about him, but for some reason this time I just felt done – cue Beyonce, boy BYE[14]. I actually thanked her, left school, and immediately broke up with him. I'll save you the drama filled details because that's really not the point. The point is that I wasn't even sad about it. I felt lighter and relieved and it was the first time in over two years that I felt empowered other than when I was on stage dancing. It was the first step in two years that I had made toward loving myself (and might I add, high school years are like dog years so basically a lifetime). He begged me to give him another chance for a really long time but the instant I had made the decision to break up with him, I had already transformed into a person I liked again and I didn't want to go back. Sometimes, I think that is why I am so strong willed now. I know that the only person who can advocate for me and make a real difference in my situation is me, no matter how much someone loves you or tries to tell you what is best in a situation, only you can actually change your own mindset and you have to WANT to make the change. My mom really disliked my boyfriend and now being a mom myself, I can understand why. She would never tell me what to do about it and would be there when I was upset even though I am sure she wanted to shake me out of it. Unfortunately, you always have to learn these things on your own and make that choice for yourself.

A few years later, I started dating my now husband,

---

14 - LOL

Desric. He has always treated me amazingly well and has been there for me through my ups and downs. I remember one time we were at my place and he saw a picture on my shelf of me with one of my friends from high school and told me 'you look really good in that picture'. Nice compliment, right? HELL, NO. How dare he comment that I looked beautiful in a photo from a time when I was completely emotionally broken! Could he not tell from looking at the picture how much that girl was picking herself apart? How insensitive of him to tell me I look good. I unleashed the full on rage and felt so offended that he thought I looked good in that snippet of time, considering I had stopped dancing competitively and had gained weight since. Spoiler alert, I didn't really fully love myself yet. Guess what though, he didn't break up with me! I heard that guys like girls that are a little crazy so I guess it's partly true (kidding, kidding). But seriously – we did get married. Despite all of my insecurities and my baggage, he still loved me and we still got married. My husband is truly a great man. He balances my high strung personality and supports me through whatever I feel I need to do for me. That, my friends, is what really matters in life. Loving yourself and having a partner, friends, and family that support you loving yourself.

Having children changes your body immensely and the whole experience for me wasn't necessarily the happy-go-lucky time I was expecting. It took us a long time to get pregnant with my first son, which led me to extreme lows on the self-love meter and constant questioning of my body's abilities and what was "wrong with me". This is not the greatest headspace to be in and when I finally did get pregnant, we had a major scare where I thought I miscarried. As it turns out, I had a sub-chorionic hemorrhage and the baby was fine, but the remainder of the pregnancy was filled with health scares and me wishing the pregnancy would be over so that he would be here and finally safe. My anxiety was through the roof the entire time and I felt like any negative thought I had was actually hurting my unborn baby, which, I felt, made me the worst parent ever with a body that wasn't even doing what it was supposed to do. It was an uphill battle until he was born. Becoming a mom was the single most empowering moment of my life and the respect I gained for myself and my body in that delivery room made me feel like I could literally do anything. That's what I mean about the self-love journey, it really is a journey. No matter how much you love yourself, there can always be things that shake your confidence and mindset. The important thing is having the tools and support to make you come back to love.

Watching my son grow and learn knowing that I created that life was truly amazing. I knew when he was six months old that I wanted another child, despite what I had been through with his pregnancy. Once we started trying for our second baby we got pregnant surprisingly quickly and were really excited. Unfortunately, though, I miscarried at 11 weeks. We were devastated and I had a really rough few months ahead as I mentally worked through the loss. A loss like that can be really difficult on a marriage and it can be really difficult to feel understood. When you feel that kind of pain, you wonder how your partner who isn't carrying that baby could ever feel how you do. It can cause resentment and I'm not going to lie, it did for me. My husband was obviously hurting and supported me the best way he could. Everyone has their own way to work toward healing, and he let me lash out, be a bitch when I felt like I was losing ground, and totally breakdown when I needed to (and sometimes still do). For that, I am grateful.

Despite what happened, a few months later we decided to try again. I got pregnant with my daughter. The pregnancy was almost exactly the same as my son's pregnancy in the sense that I had the same medical issues, extra hospital visits and guilt…most of all the guilt. I felt guilty that I wasn't connected to the pregnancy because I was too afraid of having another miscarriage. I felt guilty that I was too tired to give my son my full attention. I felt guilty that I was pregnant when I had just lost a baby 6 months before. I felt guilty that I was running a business with Jerrica but I couldn't help her do anything at trade shows because I wasn't allowed to lift or do anything physical. Just so much heavy guilt ALL the time. To be honest, if it wasn't for Jerrica, our business probably would not have continued for this last year and a half. She was (and is!) truly my rock in business and my shoulder to cry on, as not only my sister, but as my best friend. She never complained about doing it all on her own while I almost completely stepped back. I don't know how I got so lucky to have the kind of relationship we have as sisters, but having her do so much with the business while I was in and out of it mentally gave me just enough of a distraction to get me through after such a loss. It's not the first time Jerrica has lead me through a rough patch, and I know it won't be the last. When I forgot how to love myself due to circumstance, she stuck by me and reminded me what I love to do and helped me pour my attention back to our passion project, our business.

After having my daughter, I again felt safe and happy and empowered. Despite all the obstacles, despite my guilt and despite my lack of self-love throughout that 9 months, I had created another beautiful baby and my body pulled through once again. I should really just have a bit of trust in this old body of mine, shouldn't I?

The funny thing about kids is, they aren't even trying but they make you see the world and yourself in such a different light. They make you remember the magic of just having the privilege to be alive in this amazing body that functions and allows you to move and experience. Kids have belly rolls, chunky thighs, their hair is stuck up weird ways, if they even have any hair at all. They have cute little gaps in their teeth and you know what – they don't care! They care about laughing and making you laugh. They love themselves, they love all the cool things their body can do. They love looking at their goofy faces in the mirror and they LOVE sticking out their bellies. We could really learn a lot from kids and I truly look at my own kids every day to remind me how awesome I already am. I made these little self-loving creatures, after all.

Starting the business that Jerrica and I have has been so amazing and is truly a passion project. The focus we put in results in growth in our business. Truly believing in something and loving what you do is the best feeling. Going from knowing nothing about the industry to teaching ourselves what we need to know to grow a business is the ultimate feeling of empowerment. I feel so lucky to be able to do what we do and with my sister and best friend.

To be honest, writing this chapter has been quite a healing experience. Sometimes, you know things about yourself but they are just quietly sitting there, up in your headspace. Once you get them out on paper, it's like you clear it from your mind to make room for more love and peace. Writing this has me feeling pretty vulnerable and exceptionally alive at the same time. It has made me love myself more than I did before I started and has taught me how important it is to continue to love myself for so many reasons every single day.

I have worked to forgive myself for what I felt like were wasted years of my life. Years where I had shut people out to make someone else happy and lost out on experiences. I now realize that the experiences I had were actually exactly the right ones to lead me to the path I am on. Just because I know this and have worked toward continued love for myself, doesn't mean that I don't have lows and times when I lose that feeling for a little while. It is a work In progress and a lot of times I have to take a step back and remind myself why I should love me for me.

JERRICA

When I was first asked to be a part of this, I was a little bit nervous. For as long as I can remember, I have been the shy one. I'm not one to talk about myself, or be the centre of attention. I have experienced having basically 0% confidence in myself in the past. Not 10%, or 50%, but 0%. It has taken me a long time to figure it out, but I think I'm finally starting to get the hang of this whole "Eff it, I'm a boss ass b*tch" feeling, and *actually* believing it.

Growing up, I always loved and played sports. Competitive softball was my sport and I was damn good at it. I played centre field position, and when I was on the field I felt unstoppable, powerful and totally in my element. During this time, I was the most confident I have ever been. I was constantly working out, attending practices, and was part of an amazing team. They were like a family to me and it was so comforting to feel the respect and love we had for each other. There was no judgement and only encouragement. I got to travel all over Canada and the United States, which was another amazing perk of playing a high level sport. That experience gave me a chance to embrace so much positivity at such a young age and I will be forever grateful for it. Being a part of something like that was so amazing and I know that that time in my life helped to shape me into who I have become. It made me love the person I was and gave me no reason to question myself or my abilities.

Cut to 14-year-old me, heading into high school. Grade

9. It was like a whole new world. Don't get me wrong, I loved high school. I had an amazing group of friends; I actually enjoyed a lot of my classes; and didn't mind going to school - most days, anyway. That being said, I couldn't shake the all-consuming feelings of pressure: trying to fit in and be good enough, smart enough, pretty enough, skinny enough, etc. It was something I hadn't felt the year before in my small elementary school and I definitely did not feel that way when I was playing Softball.

To confirm my feelings of insecurity, I quickly learned that not everything was as it seemed within my friend groups. I remember specifically one day going and sitting with a group of friends that I didn't normally sit with and I was shocked to hear the conversations happening. One of the group's "best friends" happened to be away that day and about 90% of the conversation that happened over the lunch break was the group talking poorly about her. Judging her clothing, her personality, and just who she was as a person. I couldn't believe it and it made me think to myself, *what is said about me when I am not around? What am I doing, saying, wearing that is going to make them talk about me when I'm not there?* It perpetuated my feelings of wanting to fit in. It's experiences like those that shaped the pressure I felt every day to be someone other people approved of. Constant questioning of myself became routine, and this was a major contributor to the start of my anxiety. I was constantly trying to be perfect and fit in. There were a lot of ups and downs in how I felt about myself over those 4 years in high school, but without this time in my life, I wouldn't be the woman that I am today. Leaving high school is like leaving one world and entering to this vast new world where you can make so many more choices that aren't judged. You aren't forced to be in a certain group to be accepted and finding my own groove after high school really boosted my confidence in myself and made me realize that I really do love who I am.

A day that changed my life was a doctor's appointment where I was diagnosed with Polycystic Ovarian Syndrome (PCOS). For anyone that doesn't know, this is a disorder that primarily affects your hormones. At first, I had NO idea what it was and I had never heard anyone talk about it. It was the most frustrating thing to deal with when I found out because I literally had no one that could tell me about it from personal experience. All I had to go off of was the internet, which as we all know, is the worst place to search for medical information. It was also very frustrating because it is a disorder that affects your reproductive system. It can cause infertility and multiple symptoms that would affect my everyday life. I was having almost non-existent periods, experiencing weight gain, my energy levels seemed low, and all I could think to myself was: *What's wrong with me? Why is this happening to me? Why is my body doing this to me?* It is a horrible feeling to know that you didn't do anything to cause your diagnosis, and it's just something that you have to deal with.

Around the time that I found out that I had it was also the time that I quit playing sports. To go from working out, practicing, and playing a competitive sport every day, to basically no activity... obviously was a big shock to my system and I felt it, physically and mentally. I was around 18 years old and I went from feeling great, to feeling tired, gaining weight, and just not feeling like myself. Having PCOS just perpetuated these feelings and although the doctor told me some ways to support and manage the disorder, I just didn't feel motivated to help myself stay on top of it. Seeing other people that didn't have to deal with the same thing as me, or didn't have to worry about their hormones making them gain weight, made me upset and angry. I had a "poor me" attitude for so long, but I always had my sister to tell me to get my shit in gear and do something to better my health. We kind of both do that for each other even to this day. When we whine to each other and say we don't want to do something, we tend to push each other to get that thing done that we didn't want to do. Don't get me wrong, I still have my "poor me" days, but I try my best to snap out of it and get shit done. I am realizing all that I have to offer and that I am so much more than just this part of my story.

I have learned tools to help me with this condition and know where to find resources, which has made me feel empowered. Since being diagnosed, there have been a lot more people, even from a celebrity standpoint, that are starting to talk about PCOS. Hearing their stories has really helped me to feel less alone and to have more of a positive outlook. I have changed my mindset and understand that this is not my fault and there are lots of things I can do to manage it and take it into my own hands. I love myself despite some bad days I may have.

I honestly attribute a lot of why I am the way that I am to my sister. Not only is she my sister, she is my best friend and I look up to her SO much. I was always the annoying little sister following her around, wanting to do everything (and I mean *everything)* with her. The five-year age gap doesn't seem like anything now, but I couldn't imagine her trying to deal with my annoying little self every day when we were younger. I have also never met someone that has gone through so much in life and still has so much confidence. She is literally the definition of a badass bitch and I have learned so much from her. Sometimes I feel like I did when I was a little girl, trying to be just like her so I can get to that level of confidence and self-love that I see shine through her. I'm getting there, slowly but surely!

I am so happy now to have this company that we have created together[15]. We have always had a goal to do something together, we just couldn't figure out what that something would be. It has been a whirlwind for sure, but believe me when I say, the small shop community is something that I can't even begin to describe. I have never seen such a large group of women that are so supportive of one another and boost each other up every day. It is like its own little world and we are so lucky to be a part of it. Being self-taught in our industry is something that has given me so much confidence in myself. We started by not knowing anything two years ago, and are starting to grow

15 www.shopeverydayhustle.com

something really incredible and I am so proud of myself for stepping out of my comfort zone.

I am finding myself letting go of my insecurities more and more. The small things that used to make me nervous or would make me shut down and not move forward are not holding me back and I love the person I am continuing to grow into. I have never loved myself the way that I do now.

We hope even one bit of either of our journeys was relatable and helpful for you. When coming together to write this, we both agreed that we feel that the more you love yourself, the easier relationships are, the easier decisions are, the easier and happier life becomes. Over the years, we have both had so many ups and downs. Misunderstandings with ourselves. Times when we haven't been self-aware and times when we have blamed others for the way we feel or our own reactions.

Everyone is going to go through hardships in their lives. Your relationship with yourself is the most important relationship you will have ever have. How you treat yourself is laying the groundwork for what you feel is acceptable behaviour for others to treat you. Self-love – it's not always easy, but it is worth the work. Whatever that work is – therapy, exercise, no exercise, ice cream, vegetables, WHATEVER - you are worth it.

KEY TAKEAWAY

Kerstin Foster and Jerrica Irwin

@everyday.hustle
@momfidentaf
#selfloveclub

EPILOGUE

Courtney St Croix

Okay. Wow. That was emotional, wasn't it? The thing I love most about this project, is that no matter what story an author was telling, I could empathize with it and *feel* for her journey, even if I hadn't been through it myself. What is most poignant in my experience creating and then reading this book, is that as women, mothers, and sisters, we are fucking *resilient*. Aren't we!? We overcome trauma, difficult relationships, mental health stresses, childbirth, abuse, and hella difficult life experiences, and we have the capacity to turn these things into lessons and grow through them, instead of allowing them to seep into our definition. *That* is truly powerful.

No matter what you're going through; no matter what stage you're in currently; no matter where you are on the self-love scale at this very moment… we are all in this together. There is something so powerful about a group of women working together in support of one another, and that's exactly what this project's purpose is.

I encourage you to consider your own self-love journey after reflecting on so many different versions of how self-love can manifest. It has to start somewhere, and as you've read, it can come from many different experiences. Self-love often comes from going through difficult experiences, and seeing how strong you really are - strong enough to survive the hard parts and come out the other side.

MOMFIDENT AF has always been an outlet for me; a place where I shared my difficulty in order to help another woman along her own journey, and a place where I could share resources that help women feel damn good about themselves, exactly as they are. As the brand and community grew, I realized that I wanted to impact women in more ways than just photos and captions; I wanted to implore women to experiment with their own voices and to become published authors. I am so grateful to have gone on this journey with each and every one of the incredible authors in this inaugural co-authored project, and the authors following their lead in "Self Love Club (Vol II)" and "5 Lessons Learned Through Motherhood".

Keep your eyes peeled for future collaborative book projects, and for more information (or to apply to be a writer in a future project) you can dig deeper by going to GetMomfidentAF.com and finding the "Co-Author" page.

Thank you for walking this journey with us. We are stronger together. Always.

About the Publisher

Courtney St Croix is a 5x Best-Selling Author, Top-Rated Podcast Host, Mindset Transformation Coach, and CEO of boutique publishing house MOMFIDENT AF Media. In 2015, Courtney set out on a personal journey to whole-body self-acceptance, as she recovered from the ultimate female body transformation experience of pre- and post-pregnancy.

Courtney created the Best-Selling "#MomfidentAF Self-Love Journal" in 2018, a similar journal for adolescent girls in 2019, and has since published two other works dedicated to helping women learn to embrace their now and evolve to new levels. She is author of MOMFIDENT AS F*CK, a 5x #1 Best-Seller that released in February 2020. She leads group authorship projects through MOMFIDENT AF Media to allow women to share their own stories of self-love, and chats about confidence and motherhood on her top-rated show, The Momfidence Podcast.

Courtney lives in Ontario, Canada with her husband Chris, daughter Presley and colossal dog, Molson.

GetMomfidentAf.com | @momfidentaf | @momfidentaf.media
#MOMFIDENTAF #MOMFIDENTAFBOOK

For more on MOMFIDENT AF, co-authoring, confidence resources and access to the MOMFIDENT AF Blog, Podcast and Online

Courses, check out **GetMomfidentAF.com**

Manufactured by Amazon.ca
Bolton, ON

12990102R00186